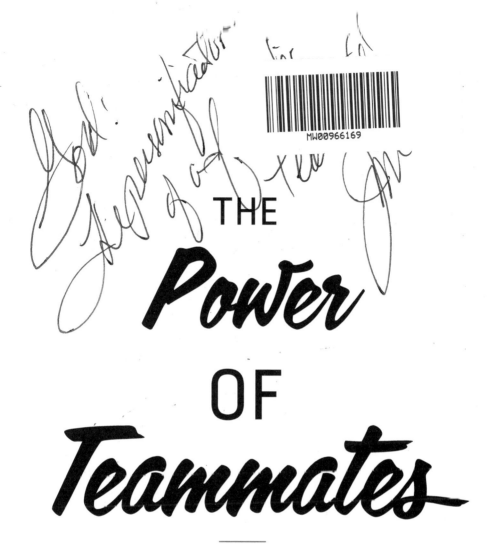

THE
Power
OF
Teammates

HOW TO LIVE BETTER
AND GET WHAT
YOU WANT FASTER!

ROGER LAJOIE, CHRIS DE PIERO & JIM ROONEY

 FriesenPress

Suite 300 - 990 Fort St
Victoria, BC, V8V 3K2
Canada

www.friesenpress.com

ISBN
978-1-5255-9953-8 (Hardcover)
978-1-5255-9952-1 (Paperback)
978-1-5255-9954-5 (eBook)

1. SELF-HELP, MOTIVATIONAL & INSPIRATIONAL

Distributed to the trade by The Ingram Book Company

TABLE OF CONTENTS

INTRODUCTION

By Roger Lajoie

D o you have any serious addictions? I have one. I was addicted for many years to self-help books.

I read them all…hundreds of them, in fact. I read self-help books from all of the "big names" in the industry, and I read some from unknown authors as well. Basically if the word "Happiness" or "Success" was in the title I would read it. I was a sucker for them.

I'm not making fun of the industry, although it sure sounds like it. I am making fun of myself.

Hey, many of these books were very helpful to me as I look back on them. I should amend that to say that most of these books were extremely helpful to me. There is a lot to be garnered from any book that is dedicated to making your life better, making you happier and helping you in any area of self-improvement. Anyone who writes a book that in any way, shape or form attempts to make the reader more successful and able to live a better life deserves applause in my mind.

Some of these books are actually excellent reads full of good information and advice to help you help yourself. I purged my house of my more than 2,000 book collection recently, but I did keep several hundred of my favorites and most of them are in this self-help genre. And as much as I sometimes make fun of my addiction to them, I just couldn't bear to part with many of these "permanent keeper" books while I did my much-needed purge, some of which I've already read multiple times.

I'm not alone in my addiction to these books. There are all kinds of people who are also addicted to self-help books. Perhaps you are one of them, and perhaps that's why you have turned to this book and the TEAMMATES program.

The fact that so many of us read personal improvement books explains why there are thousands of self-help books in any bookstore or online at any given time. Everybody wants to be better. Everybody wants to be happier. Everybody wants to improve and have success. Sure we do. And most of us are also looking for quick answers, so when a book comes with the promise of "This book will make you 100% happier in 10 minutes" well of course addicts like me are going to jump at reading it…and so will my fellow addicts.

As an aside, the late great comedian George Carlin had a funny line about finding self-help books in the bookstore.

"I'd show you where the self-help section was, but that would defeat the purpose."

That pretty much says it all when it comes to our preoccupation with this kind of reading. We want somebody else to help us help ourselves. Oh the irony of that!

All jokes aside however, any positive reading material which does indeed help you help yourself is a good thing. I learned a lot from these books over the years, and I think most people get a lot out of them too.

There is just one problem with these books, however, and it's a big one. **They are not enough.**

As great as they are to read, as great as some of the information in them is, as great as many of the writers are, they still somehow leave us lacking. That's why we need to read so many of them; they are all helpful to a point but not ONE of them is helpful to the point where we can stop reading ALL of them.

If these books really did deliver as promised, making us happier, more successful and all-round more improved, we wouldn't need to read hundreds of them, would we? After a few of the really good ones, shouldn't we be all set? And as much as I do truly love this genre of writing, I find so much of the material in many of these books repetitive. Don't you?

These books are clearly not enough to make us feel satisfied. We often finish one and just go on to the next, thinking we are not doing enough to improve our lives the way we want to, so we better read another one. What then is missing?

Here's what's missing. As great as any self-help book that caters to the masses is, it can't help any of us deal with our *specific* problems in our *specific* situations. I don't mean this as a criticism because it's simply not possible for any book to do that. Books aren't written for individuals, they are written for the masses. They have to be. A book only about your specific problems would only be bought by you.

The messages in these books are positive. They are useful. They can help us to be happier and more successful to a certain extent. But they are all-encompassing, and therefore they aren't tailored to us as individuals. They are generic. They have to be.

The logical answer to that dilemma is that along with reading these great books, we should find a mentor or coach who can help us address our specific concerns and work with us on our individual and unique circumstances.

Yeah right, many of you are thinking. That costs a lot of money. And while you can get the latest self-help bestseller for maybe $25, the services of a Life Coach can be much more expensive and beyond the budgets of a lot of people.

The sad reality is that the kind of people who could really benefit from having a coach or mentor in their lives are the same kind of people who can't afford the price tag of Tony Robbins or another high profile coach to work with them individually.

This certainly presents quite a dilemma. The obvious next step for anyone who has read even only one or two self-help books, never mind hundreds, is to get some individualized coaching. But I understand the high price tag that excellent coaches command – they are in high demand and they need to be compensated properly for their time because one-on-one coaching is time consuming and it's not easy.

I know. I've used the services of a Life Coach and for the last seven years have worked as a Personal Development Coach myself.

It is the classic "between a rock and a hard place" scenario – excellent life coaches make more money pushing out change-your-life books and holding expensive seminars than they would ever do by coaching individuals.

However many people don't get to the next level of their personal development without someone to help them focus in on their individual problems. The books and seminars are great, but they just aren't *specific* enough.

The majority of my working career has been spent as a sports broadcaster, writer and hockey team executive, a 41 year run that has been more fun than work for me if the truth be told. But I have always had an interest in teaching and mentoring people, especially students, along the way in my career.

I was also a teacher for more than a decade at Ryerson University and the College of Sports Media. After my extremely positive experience working with a Life Coach nearly 20 years ago, I always felt that coaching and mentoring on a formal level is something I would enjoy doing as my sports media career stated winding down.

So that's what I did. In 2013 I started taking on some clients, charging them a very reasonable fee since most of them were former students of mine. I worked with them on their specific areas of concern. It was rewarding for me and for them, and a wonderful way for me to give something back after all I had been given.

However personal development coaching was not feasible as a business for me, especially at the height of my sports media career. To make individual coaching work, the price tag has to be much higher than I was charging. I wasn't going to raise prices dramatically – I wasn't comfortable doing it – and frankly I didn't want to only coach rich people. However I also could not afford to continue investing the huge amount of time required to properly work with my clients at the current rate I was charging. That was another dilemma.

Even though I had also written three successful books, I had no desire to start churning out my own "secrets to a successful life" series of books to earn a living. No disrespect to anyone doing that, but that was not for me – the world does not need any more generic self-help books in the bookstore; there are already too many of them for even an addict to read.

What I believed people needed was cost-effective individualized coaching to go along with whatever book they were reading. People needed a program that would give them broadly based information, but also with a personal touch. For it to be as accessible to as many people as possible, it had to be priced affordably, yet priced high enough to make it worth the time of the coach/mentor. Personal Development Coaching (that's what I call it), requires a lot of time and effort for both the coach and the client.

Honestly, I racked my brains for years wrestling with this dilemma. How could I take the elements of great self-development books, boil them down into a user friendly course, and also provide clients with the same individual attention they needed to make the most of working with a PDC?

The answer was – I couldn't do it, at least not alone. I needed something first.

What I needed were good people to help me. What I needed were people who had skills in areas where I was lacking a bit. What I needed were teammates.

I found them. Jim Rooney, former owner of the Guelph Storm of the Ontario Hockey League and high school principal, and Chris De Piero, former General Manager/Coach of the Oshawa Generals of the OHL and Athletic Director at Toronto's St. Michael's College School.

I'm Roger Lajoie, sports broadcaster/writer/executive, three-time author and teacher. Jim, Chris and I are your Personal Development Coaches now via this book and program. This isn't just another book, if you work the exercises in it with us and then allow us to help you deal with your specific needs.

This is the program the three of us developed to help you improve your life. The information in the book may be generic, but the feedback we provide with it is specific to you when you work with us on these exercises.

We certainly hope you will do that – or work on them with another mentor or coach that you trust. We can do so much more when we work with others than we can when we work alone.

Welcome to TEAMMATES. We are so happy to have you on our team!

WISDOM NUGGET #1: Your life's journey is much easier and a lot more fun if you don't travel alone.

WHAT WE DO

The three of us started our TEAMMATES venture on June 10, 2019. We met that day at the historic Maple Leaf Gardens (now called the Mattamy Athletic Centre) at Ryerson University in Toronto. We decided that we all felt the same way – we were at the stage of our lives and careers that we wanted to give something back. This program you are about to go through was our way to do that.

I had been doing my Life Development Coaching for five years by that time and had more than 50 clients over that period. Jim and Chris hadn't done any formal coaching, but both were widely known as mentors, teachers and coaches throughout their careers.

Find a void and fill it. Everybody says that and everybody is right – if you can do that you are filling a need. The existing void we examined was between the self-help book industry and the pricy individual Life Coach… there was no in-between from what we could see.

So we started working together. In our first 12 months, we produced 365 daily inspirational tweets, published 15 blogs and recorded 15 podcasts. We did this on our own time and for everybody to get something out of the messages we were sending. We made these products available online for free.

That body of work forms a lot of the nucleus of this course. I am the writer of the group, so I did the tweets, the blog and this book. Jim and Chris are the educators – they developed the course questions that accompany the material. We did the podcasts together, and we combined our efforts designing this program for you to work through. It's not just another self-help book you are reading, or another series of podcasts, or just a life coaching program. It's all three. It's valuable generic information with specific feedback for you and your issues - when you work with us.

Even if you aren't a TEAMMATE, this book can be valuable to your personal growth. But we highly recommend you discuss the material here with a coach, mentor or friend that can help you with your specific issues. You'll get much better results that way.

This book is a course that you work through by doing all the exercises contained in it. If you are in the TEAMMATES program you'll be working with one of our associates. If you aren't, find someone you know and trust to fulfill that role for you. That component will help you take the generic material and apply it to your specific needs.

Everybody needs teammates. We don't accomplish anything of real significance without them. What I couldn't do alone, I found I could do with my TEAMMATES. We are confident that by working through these exercises with a mentor, you'll get the full value of the lessons they contain.

Are you ready to go? Then let's get going and start making your life better right now!

THE COURSE

We begin our journey together with you by you doing some work. We are your TEAMMATES and we are very confident that with us helping you, you are going to come out of this program far more prepared to handle the challenges of your life than you were before you took it. Whether you are working with us or using another partner, how much you get out of this program is directly proportional to how much you are willing to work it.

The course begins with a simple questionnaire so you can see where you are at right now in your life (the questionnaire is coming shortly). We have used this short questionnaire with all of our clients over the years with great results, as it really gets you thinking about what you really want, and gets your coach/mentor thinking about the best way to help you when you do your individual work.

Answer the questionnaire honestly. Take your time with it. This is not a test, there are no wrong answers. Once we get into the individual part of the program, these answers will give the mentor you are working with a running start on how he or she can best help you become better…faster!

There are lots of different names for the kind of coaching/mentoring that we do, but ours is simply this – we are PERSONAL DEVELOPMENT COACHES and this program is geared toward helping you by outlining general principles for you to consider via the course work. We then follow that up with personal one-on-one mentoring (again please do the same whether you are working with TEAMMATES coaches or not).

There are several guiding principles that we adhere to throughout this program. To begin with, don't expect TEAMMATES Life Development Coaches (or whoever you are using as a mentor) to solve your problems for you; they are here to help you to develop the skills and tools that you need to solve your own problems, whatever they may be.

The main thing a PDC does is this: we remind you of what you already know, and work with you to apply that knowledge. To be honest, most of us know what we need to do to live a more successful life, right? We have to work harder. We need to develop a strong mindset. We need to be persistent in our efforts. This hardly comes as a shock to anyone! But a PDC can keep you on track and keep you accountable for your actions. A good mentor will be looking to help you close the gap between what you know, and what you do about what you know.

Good coaches observe behavior, help clients formulate a plan and give feedback on the results of that plan's implantation. Mentors will also tell you what you need to hear when you need to hear it, so make sure whomever you are working with is going to be honest with you.

The three authors of this book have more than 120 combined years of business experience, as teachers, writers, broadcasters, principals, coaches, managers, owners and administrators. We are all at the stage of our lives and careers where it is time for us to direct our energies towards passing along that experience and wisdom we have gained in so many different ways to you. We know that working through this program with us, or another trusted mentor you have in your life, will produce results for you.

When the student is ready, the teacher appears. This program will be extremely useful to you but only if you work hard at it. The biggest impediment to learning, we all believe, is people not being open to learning. Even with our 120 years of experience, we are always learning. So if you think you know it all already sorry – we can't help you.

Make your decision now before you get too far into this – are you a know-it-all or are you a learn-it-all?

If you are honestly ready to learn, then you are ready to get started with this.

It takes as much effort to live an unproductive life as it does to live a productive one. A problem shared is a problem halved, and having TEAMMATES in your corner can provide you with mentorship and help you learn some new skills to use in tackling life's challenges, both personally and professionally.

So let's begin with you filling out the questionnaire, and let's start giving you the benefits of having TEAMMATES in your corner!

NOTE – **If you are using your own coach/mentor, please skip this section and head straight to STEP ONE: WORKING WITH OUR BLOGS**

> WISDOM NUGGET #2: You are either working to make your dreams come true, or working for somebody else's dreams to come true.

The following is our TEAMMATES rundown. If you are using your own mentor, fill out these questions and give them to your coach before you begin!

PERSONAL DEVELOPMENT COACHING PROGRAM

TEAMMATES INTRODUCTION

Hello! We are very happy to be working with you for the next month, helping you to help yourself with your personal development. You have a Coach now, a Mentor or just a Teammate if you prefer. Call it whatever you want, labels are not important. The bottom line – we are in your corner to help you discover how you can be better in whatever area of your life you want to improve in. That is what personal development is all about.

As an introduction to our working together, we'd like to introduce the three partners in our Personal Development Coaching organization – TEAMMATES. The three of us work together making sure we hold ourselves accountable to YOU in this process.

TEAMMATES TRIO

Starting on June 10, 2019, Chris De Piero, Jim Rooney and Roger Lajoie became TEAMMATES, as we look to help coach and mentor more people to be the best they can be – our tag lines are BE OUTSTANDING! BEST ALWAYS! LOOK FOR GOOD!

We would be delighted if you could follow us on Twitter (@TeammatesTrio), and on our Facebook page (@TeammatesTrio). You can also find us on the Triumph Sports Communications website: www.rogerlajoie.com.

We send out daily messages on Twitter and our Facebook page to help inspire and keep our community of like-minded thinking people motivated. We also post regular blogs on various life improvement strategies, and do a regular audio podcast. The three of us all have one thing in common – we have been truly blessed in our careers and want to pass on what we have learned to help you.

CHRIS DE PIERO has been an educator in various forms for the past 26 years, as a teacher and coach. He has been the Director of Athletics at St. Michael's College School as well as a classroom teacher. He played professional hockey in Italy before becoming an accomplished hockey coach, leading the St. Michael's Buzzers to back-to-back Ontario titles before moving on to the Ontario Hockey League. Chris was Assistant Coach, Assistant General Manager, Head Coach and General Manager with the Oshawa Generals from 2006-12, and worked as an Amateur Scout for the Pittsburgh Penguins from 2012-16. He recently returned to North America after serving as Assistant Coach with Hockey Club Lugano in Switzerland, and is once again working for St. Michael's College School in an administrative role. BE OUTSTANDING!

JIM ROONEY has been a fixture in Guelph sports for decades. He was co-owner, president and governor of the Ontario Hockey League's Guelph Storm from 1991-2006, and Chairman of the Board of Governors of the OHL from 1995-2001. His Guelph teams won two OHL titles (1998, 2004) and participated in four Memorial Cups, including one as a host city.

He later became owner of the Guelph Royals of the Intercounty Baseball League after serving as the league's Commissioner from 2001-2009. He was principal at Bishop Macdonell and Our Lady of Lourdes high schools, where many of his Guelph players attended. Jim was also co-chair of the Ontario Winter Games (2002-03), and was Educational Consultant for Team Canada's first U-18 gold medal winning team in Russia in 2003. He was elected to the Guelph Sports Hall of Fame in 2017 to recognize his outstanding contributions as a builder in Guelph sports over many decades. BEST ALWAYS!

ROGER LAJOIE has been working in the sports media field for more than four decades. He has been a reporter, editor, broadcaster, announcer, author, teacher and hockey executive at various times in his career. He taught at Ryerson University in the Sports Media program for four years and was a teacher at the College of Sports Media from 2008-18. He wrote the biography of Canadian hockey legend Paul Henderson among his three published books, and has done more than 3,700 shows as a radio talk show host on Sportsnet 590 The Fan. He has covered more than 250 major sporting events, including 17 World Series, 14 Stanley Cup Finals, 13 Super Bowls and 11 NBA Finals. He has worked as an executive for the Canadian Hockey League, and was Vice President of both the Mississauga St. Michael's Majors of the OHL and the Belleville Senators of the AHL. For 10 seasons he has been one of the Official Scorers of the Toronto Blue Jays and has operated Triumph Sports Communications for more than 30 years. He has been personal coaching/mentoring clients for the past seven years. LOOK FOR GOOD!

Thank you all for your support and friendship. Chris, Jim and Roger look forward to having you as our TEAMMATE!

YOUR PROGRAM

We have been coaching and mentoring people all our working careers, but first started coaching/mentoring individual clients in 2013. Starting in June, 2019 the three of us teamed up to combine our efforts and energies to create this program. We have developed a 30-day program that has had tremendous results for our clients in helping them live better lives – it's really that simple. And this program is tailored exclusively for you, as we will be working one-on-one dealing with your particular areas that you feel you need to improve on. There is some work involved here, but we're confident you'll enjoy the program we're about to undertake together. So...let's begin!

RUNDOWN

Once you have answered the five questions, our team will assess your answers and discuss ways we feel we can help you individually. Since 2013 we have refined this course several times to ensure it makes the best use of your time and our time. It's a format that has worked very well in the past and continues to for both clients and for Roger, Chris and Jim.

Here is our rundown for TEAMMATES:

1. **Answer the questionnaire.** Make your answers as long or as short as you feel like, the length isn't important. These questions will set the tone for our first meeting and the direction we will take over the following 30 days, how we will focus and frame our discussions.
2. **First meeting.** We will schedule a first meeting (60 minutes) where we will go over your questionnaires and establish what we will accomplish in the coming time we spend together.
3. **Weekly web chat.** We will provide some feedback and some suggestions to you after the first meeting, and once a week we will chat online for 30 minutes at a mutually agreed time to monitor your progress and provide more feedback. That's four meetings, one per week.
4. **Final meeting and assessment.** If it's possible to meet in person for this – great. If not, online works as well. As part of the continuing coaching commitment we will also be available by email for the next six months, whenever some "fine tuning" is required.

QUESTIONNAIRE

OK! So before our first meeting please answer the following questions and send them back to us by email at teammates@rogers.com. Again – no particular length of answer required, just be honest in your replies.

- Q1 – Describe briefly how you think your life is going right now. How are you feeling about where you are?
- Q2 – What do you think a Coach/Mentor can help you the most with?
- Q3 –What's the biggest challenge you face now, or obstacle you want to overcome, or area you need to improve in?
- Q4 – What's the best thing about your life at the present moment? What's going really well for you?
- Q5 – Are you willing to look at your life in a completely different way, or do you think that's not necessary?

Please send your answers back before our first meeting. We look forward to watching this program work for you as it has for many other clients in the past seven years. Now it is time for you to get to work on the course in this book to work on general principals.

NEXT STEPS

Once we receive your questionnaire the work begins at our end as well. Jim and Chris have developed a syllabus which you will follow during the four weeks we have together.

This book is required reading material for all of our clients as it serves several purposes. First – it introduces us fully to you and let's you how the actual mentoring works.

Second, the 10 blogs and 365 daily tweets act as a starting guide for study. All of our blogs are based on the most common challenges many people are facing with their lives and careers. And although this course is directed at helping YOU tackle YOUR challenges, we feel that by starting you off with reading these blogs and our accompanying comments, you will see several topics that will resonate with YOU.

Make notes about them. Really look to understand the points we are covering in them. These blogs, along with our accompanying audio series, will get you thinking about better ways to approach your problems, change your mindset, and get you on the road to having a better life.

We include the tweets for several purposes. First – feel free to use them yourself! We felt that sending out a daily motivational message was something we wanted to do because simply it is the right thing to do. We will continue to provide these messages on an ongoing basis, but our complete first year of tweeting is included in this book for you to enjoy…and retweet if you like!

Second – we have found many times that you never know what message will strike a chord with someone and really resonate with them. This course is all about you working with us to improve your life through our personal development program, but if a single tweeted message – or multiple messages – helps rewire your thinking immediately, that is just terrific.

Third – we believe that reading these tweeted messages one after another will lift your spirits. We are strong believers in the spreading of powerful messages, so that's why we want you to read them all – and then pass them around. Wisdom shared is wisdom doubled…and in the case of social media, it might even be wisdom going viral.

To review: You start by filling out the questionnaire. You read this book completely. You meet with one of us to complete the course via email and an accompanying audio program. We continue to keep in touch with you via email for the next six months to check in on a regular basis.

And most importantly, once you have completed our course, we are TEAMMATES for life. Together we can do so much more than we can do alone!

Use this book as we go along in our journey together. Jim, Chris or Roger (whoever your PDC is) will be referring to it throughout our time working together. Absorb the lessons the blogs talk about, and see which ones most resonate with you. You will also have an audio file featuring our podcasts that will help you explore other topics that may especially resonate with you.

Listen to the entire audio file. Make notes on the topics discussed that pertain to your specific challenges. Jim, Chris or Roger will then work with you on your issues after you have read and listened to our general offerings.

> ## WISDOM NUGGET #3: Chase down your goals like you're running after the last bus of the night.

TESTIMONIALS

Before we go any further into the material, we want to offer testimonials from two of Roger's clients that are still our TEAMMATES today. Once you have completed this course, you are a TEAMMATE for life and we want you to see what other clients have thought about the process.

We include these testimonials at this point to show you that it is the individualized mentoring that comes along with this book that makes our TEAMMATES program a full self-help learning experience.

Eduardo Belmonte and Megan Sloan provided these testimonials and we present them totally unedited. As you'll see by their thoughts, the TEAMMATES program is tailored just for you and we want you to see that it's the mentoring that comes with this book and audio program that will *really* help you make breakthroughs with YOUR specific issues.

Testimonial
Eduardo Belmonte

During the month of October 2019, I had the opportunity to work with Roger as part of the TEAMMATES mentorship program. Over that time, we focused on an area of development I deemed important- Time Management, Multitasking & Planning.

Roger prefaced me before we began, asking if I was prepared to change my way of thinking and after completing the program, I now fully understand its significance. A good portion of the game is played in the mind of an athlete, and before manifesting positive output one must have mastered the mental play.

Our initial two sessions were focused on building a better picture of my current situation and professional/personal landscape for Roger. I completed a thorough questionnaire which was followed by deeper discussions where we continued to peel back more layers, identify the contradictions, and develop a plan.

This was helpful because it allowed me to take a step back and look at my life with context. I remember describing one of our conversations as a "stripping" of myself, a process I felt deeply for one simple reason - the "why." I learned its importance, and how everything is about the "why." This is especially true in entrepreneurship where asking this question can lead to a purpose driven business or life based on our true core values. With that "why" he challenged me to ask many more questions of myself.

From there we considered specific strategies - I was tasked with plotting out my schedule and recording my daily activities. This was important as it allowed me to see in real-time what I was able to accomplish throughout the week and it's a strategy that has helped me get organized for each day since then.

Having done this, I was able to rethink not only my process but the idea of "process" in general. When asked "are you enjoying this process?" it reinforced the idea that life is really about the journey not the destination, or as Roger so eloquently put, "fall in love with planning, not the plan." Things change, they don't always go as "planned" but if you fall in love with planning, you embrace the journey and can appreciate everything in between. That was strong advice that can lead to a very fulfilling life.

By "looking for good," we train our minds to consistently seek positivity in each situation. It's easy to get drawn into negativity especially if something doesn't go our way, so how we view things and our internal narrative plays a vital role in how we operate day-to-day and across every aspect of life. If you fully embrace the process, appreciating the ups and downs, find the positives by "looking for good," you'll build yourself a necessary armor.

I was faced with a situation during our mentorship where Roger's idea of removing mental roadblocks was particularly true. I had to decide whether to take a business trip to LA for a music conference that COULD yield particular benefits if I took the jump. His advice, "if money is not an issue, what do you do?"

After removing the financial, mental barrier, I decided to make the trip and reaped the benefits 10-fold.When I came back, I was very optimistic.

Overall, the program was very effective in the few short weeks I had with Roger. I developed strategies to help manage my clock, mental tactics to overcome obstacles, created context around my life and learned some fundamentals about mentoring others. My values were also reinforced by a "nudge" to dig deeper.

As a professional whose core business is also based on guidance and personal development, TEAMMATES provided layers of benefit, and I recommend it to anyone who's seriously committed to developing themselves and challenging what they thought they knew.

Additionally, Roger is an incredibly knowledgeable, insightful and motivating individual whose passion for helping others speaks magnitudes about who he is as a person and as a professional. I was honored and grateful for this opportunity.

Thank You Roger & TEAMMATES!

Eduardo Belmonte
President
AMO TALENT MANAGEMENT

Testimonial
Megan Sloan

Coming into the life coaching sessions, I was feeling a bit lost and out of control of my life and out of touch with myself.

I wasn't sure what to expect when I first started but I promised to keep an open mind and any kind of help was welcome because honestly, what did I have to lose? Now, having gone through this journey with Roger, I know that I might not have it all figured out, but now, that actually excites me!

Let me explain; Roger is a very gifted and beautiful person. He not only makes you feel heard and understood but he will never let you fall victim to your own narrative. Roger has helped me in the biggest way imaginable, in a way that I never knew I actually needed. He gave me the opportunity to change my mindset.

Not only that, but he has helped me fall in love with that process. As difficult and as messy as it is, Roger's support and listening ears paired with his endless supply of enlightened little nuggets of wisdom have profoundly impacted me and the trajectory of my life. He allowed me the space to come to conclusions on my own, make mistakes, helped dust me back off and encouraged me to try again.

The TEAMMATES program was not designed to be a series of steps that you must follow to find all the answers to life's problems. I have to admit, at the beginning, that's what I was hoping for (being the type-A person that I am). Instead, I was challenged, emboldened, and learned to listen to my intuition and stand in my truth.

It's been everything I needed and didn't know I needed. I am forever grateful for this experience and my time with Roger.

Thank you Roger and TEAMMATES!

Megan Sloan
Student, Fanshawe College
London, Ontario

WORKING WITH OUR BLOGS

We begin by studying 10 blogs that deal with various issues in your life and how to better handle them. Read the introduction to each and then work with your mentor on the questions below each one of them.

BLOG NO. 1: Solving Problems

Like most courses you are going to take anywhere, this TEAMMATES course has required reading. It's what you are reading right now!

For the past two years we have been blogging on a regular basis and we've taken 10 of these blogs and placed them here for you to read and absorb some of the general principles we believe are necessary in order to have a successful life.

Each blog covers a general topic and at the end of each one, there are three discussion points/questions for you to consider and think about – then discuss with your PDC. This will form a basis of understanding of where you are now in your thinking, both before we start working on your specific needs, during that process, and afterwards as well.

Blog No. 1 talks about how much information we now have at our fingertips. It really is amazing, especially to veterans like the three of us, how much information can be garnered in just a few seconds with a Google search in these times.

Getting answers has never been easier for us. We are one click away from finding out everything we need to know to solve many of life's problems. The most common reply we get from clients when we are teaching them material is this: "I already know that."

Congratulations to us all, we are all so smart! But since we are why is it then that we still can't seem to find the proper answers to our individual problems? Blog No. 1 talks about this issue. Please read it and then think about the three questions after it. Your PDC will be discussing these with you, and how they pertain to your problems.

We know everything! So how come we can't solve our problems better?

"Information is not knowledge."
— **Albert Einstein**

It's amazing how easy it is to get information in this era.

Just Google it!

It's so simple. We can find out anything we want, anytime we want. Just get online, just Google it and *Voila!* – everything you need to know is nicely laid out for you. It couldn't be easier...although no doubt somebody somewhere is trying to do just that, make it even easier for us.

Regardless, we live in a time where information is readily available, so much so that there is no excuse to not access it when we need it. And why wouldn't we take advantage of such an amazing storage of information at our fingertips? We'd be foolish not to.

But as Albert Einstein said – information is not knowledge. Information without application is useless. Information alone is not the answer to our problems. Correctly applying information is the answer to our problems.

We know what to do. We have access to all the information we need to solve any problem we have. We just Goggled it after all!

For example - we know what we're supposed to eat to be healthier; we know how we're supposed to handle our finances; and we know we need to work harder and smarter to advance in our careers. Yet why are so many of us struggling with health problems, money problems, and stuck in jobs we don't like without advancing forward?

It's because we lack the knowledge. We lack the wisdom. We are not applying all this information the Google monster has bestowed upon us because we are missing something very important.

> *"The problems are solved, not by giving new information,*
> *but by arranging what we have known since long."*
> **— Ludwig Wittgenstein, Philosophical Investigations**

We are missing the knowledge and wisdom to help best use that information.

Yes we can look up any information we want and have it in mere seconds, but how do we "arrange what we have known since long," as Ludwig Wittgenstein said? How do we take that information and properly apply it on a consistent basis to make life better for us and our families?

That's the tougher part. Information is not knowledge. Information is not experience. Information is not wisdom.

You can teach information, but you can't teach wisdom. That only comes from experience. And how then does one acquire wisdom?

> *"By three methods we may learn wisdom: First, by reflection,*
> *which is noblest; second, by imitation, which is easiest;*
> *and third by experience, which is the bitterest."*
> **— Confucius**

We can learn wisdom by reflection. We can learn wisdom by imitation. And we can learn wisdom by experience. Taking the time to reflect on life and gaining experience over the years dealing with life's problems makes you wise. 100 percent true.

But note what Confucius says is the EASIEST way to acquire wisdom – imitation. We can use the wisdom of people who have the knowledge and the experience that we lack to help us process all of this information we now have at our fingertips.

We can use a coach. Or use a teacher or a use a mentor. We can learn from people who have already learned what we want to know.

We would indeed be foolish not to use Google searches to get information, as it's right there for us. And we would be equally foolish not to use the services of trusted coaches, teachers and mentors when they are available to us.

If we are fortunate enough to live a long life, we will eventually spend enough time reflecting and experiencing life to acquire the wisdom we need to live it better. But none of us will ever live long enough to reflect or experience *everything* we would like to know. There is an easier (and quicker) way.

So…let's acquire wisdom the EASIEST way there is to. Let's imitate. Let's use the wisdom others have acquired for our benefit. Know why are we using quotes from these great thinkers in this blog for instance?

They acquired wisdom and are willing to share it with us.
Why wouldn't we?! "Any fool can know. The point is to understand."
— **Albert Einstein**

Ask for help when you need it. Find coaches, teachers and mentors who have gone through the reflections and experiences that have made them wise. Let them share their wisdom with you. Imitate them. One candle can light thousands of candles and its shine is not the least diminished.

Wisdom shared is wisdom doubled.

> ## WISDOM NUGGET #4: Nobody ever learned to swim by reading a book.

Discussion questions on Blog No. 1:
1. In this era of information being so widely available, why do we still seem to struggle finding answers to our problems?
2. What is the difference between knowledge and wisdom?
3. Why are so many people not willing to ask for help from people who have been where they want to go?

BLOG NO. 2: Choosing Optimism

We have already seen in our first blog that people have all the answers to life's questions at their fingertips. And here's something we all know, or certainly should know: An optimistic attitude is vital to success.

And yet again – we know this, but we sometimes don't practice it, do we? Why not? This is not pop psychology, these are facts: optimistic people live longer, they are healthier and they are much better equipped to handle their problems than negative thinkers are. So anybody in their right mind should be an optimistic person, right?

Perhaps we're not in our right minds when we don't choose to be optimistic. That's what we discuss in Blog No. 2. Again, read it and answer the three questions afterwards.

Optimism is good for your health. So why are people so pessimistic?

In his terrific book "Learned Optimism" Martin Seligman, a pioneer on the principles of positive psychology, explains the principles of optimism and how optimism is an attitude towards life that can be learned.

In other words, optimism is a choice we make.

Optimistic people are healthier and happier than those who are more prone to negativity and pessimism, and live better lives. This is not just pop psychology - this is now considered science thanks largely to the work of thought leaders like Seligman.

If you have not read his book, it comes highly recommended.

But you know this already…right? Everybody knows this. While Seligman and others who have studied the principles of positive psychology have given scientific credence to this belief, it really is just common sense – optimism is good for you. It makes you happier.

So…why are so many people pessimistic?

There are lots of reasons actually, among them the fact that there is an overwhelming negativity bias in our media. Bad news sells. It sells big time.

The worse the news is the bigger treatment it gets. So a typical "news cycle" is often one bad piece of news after another. No wonder we get depressed. No wonder we develop a negative mindset towards everything.

Want to get a quick following on social media? Spew out hatred, negativity and vitriol and you are sadly well on your way in all likelihood. Make a reasonable, thoughtful comment on an important issue and it's probably largely ignored. People are more drawn to negative comments than they are positive ones – just check the reactions in the COMMENTS section of any website for proof of that. It takes maybe 50 positive reviews to offset the review of one hater, at least in the minds of some people.

The great comedian Larry David talked about this topic once. He was at a baseball game at Yankee Stadium and was put on the Jumbotron so the crowd could see he was there, as is often the case with celebrities.

New York fans can be rough, but they responded with a standing ovation for David, which he happily acknowledged.

Leaving the game later, as he was waiting for his car to be brought to him, another car drove by. The driver rolled down his window and yelled "You suck David!" and sped off.

David's car then picked up his group and on the drive home, David complained bitterly about the one guy who yelled at him. His friends admonished him, telling him he'd gotten a standing ovation at Yankee Stadium! Why, they told him, let one guy upset you so much and ruin your night?!

Why indeed. But we are all guilty of that sometimes - focusing on the negative instead of the positive, even if the positive far outweighs the negative.

Another reason many of us don't choose optimism – we don't understand what it really is.

Optimism is not thinking everything is good. It is looking for the good in everything. Optimism is not ignoring the bad things that happen it's a way of dealing with them. Optimism is not an "unrealistic view" of the world it is very much grounded in realism.

Optimism is not Pollyanna thinking. It is a way of looking at life based on gratitude, positivity and faith. Living optimistically makes perfect sense and is really just the logical way to live.

And of course, here's the biggest reason to be optimistic:
"I have never seen a monument erected to a pessimist." – Paul Harvey

---

WISDOM NUGGET #5: Find what brings you real joy and do more of it.

Discussion questions on Blog No. 2:

1. Would you say you are an optimistic person? Do you look at life with the glass half full or half empty?
2. Why do you think people like Larry David focus on the "one bad apple" they run into instead of all the people that appreciate them? Why the negativity bias?
3. Do you find it tough to find any good in a situation that appears to be all negative?

BLOG NO. 3: Feelings Are Not Facts

We all have feelings. And those feelings really come to the forefront when we face a major adversity in life.

Human beings often have very strong feelings, and they should never be repressed. But feelings are not facts; they are just feelings about what happens to us. We sometimes forget that, and that can get us into a bad mindset.

Circumstances don't make us unhappy. It's our feelings about the circumstances that make us unhappy. When we don't get that job we really wanted, or a loved one gets sick, or when "the facts" of life come down hard on us, is when we really need to separate our feelings from our facts.

Blog No. 3 talks about realizing that we can sometimes mistake how we feel with how things really are. Read this blog and consider the talking points below once again for when your PDC discusses them with you.

Your feelings are not facts; they are just feelings!

One of the most popular television shows from decades ago was "Dragnet" featuring Jack Webb. The iconic actor played the role of Joe Friday, a police officer, who said "just the facts" when interviewing people for the cases he was working on.

Just the facts ma'am. Just the facts.

Facts are important. There are certain realities in life that must be dealt with, so dealing with "the facts of life" is a necessary skill.

But far too often we confuse our feelings with the facts. Your feelings are not facts.

Remember that…YOUR FEELINGS ARE NOT FACTS. Neither are your thoughts. Your feelings are important to deal with and recognize, and so are your thoughts, but feelings and thoughts are not facts.

It's easy to confuse them for facts however. When something bad happens, we usually wind up feeling bad and thinking bad thoughts. That's only natural.

But when a bad feeling hits you, or a bad thought hits you, stop for a moment. Breathe. And ask yourself a crucial three word question.

"Is that true?"

Assess your life and where you are right now, really examine your circumstances. Is what you are dealing with "facts" or is it feelings and thoughts? When you change the way you look at things, the things you look at change. Is what you're feeling really a fact?

Your circumstances don't make you feel sad; it's how you feel about your circumstances that make you feel sad.

Let's say you've lost your job, which is a very difficult circumstance to deal with for most of us.

Your reaction might be something like: "I lost my job. I feel horrible about that. I'm thinking I will never recover from this calamity."

Is that true? Let's separate the facts from the feeling and thoughts here.

Fact – you lost your job. That's a circumstance and it's true.

You feel horrible about it and you are thinking you will never recover from the loss.

Ask yourself – is that true?

Feelings are not facts. Thoughts are not facts. And how we feel and what we think about the circumstances (the facts) of our life is what brings on feelings of sadness and hopelessness, not the actual circumstances.

The job loss is a fact. How you react to it is a feeling and a thought, not a fact. Here is a wonderful, liberating truth - you can learn to control and examine your thoughts and feelings better. Do that and your life changes for the better.

You *can* learn to do that. That's a fact!

When you change the way you look at things, the things you look at change.

Perhaps losing the job will just lead you to find a better one. Perhaps the job was making you sick and tired and you had to get out. Perhaps when you really examine your feelings, you will realize that the feelings attached to your job loss are making you sad, not the job loss.

Two brothers lost their Mom from cancer. That is a horrible, tragic fact.

One brother went around focusing on the loss. "I feel terrible," he said. "We as a family will never recover from this loss."

The other brother had learned to examine his feelings and thoughts about everything, even such a horrible thing as losing a family member.

"We had a terrible loss," he said. "But she was in pain and now she is at peace. Remembering her will bring our family even closer together."

Pain is inevitable. Suffering is optional.

Examine your feelings and thoughts about the "facts" of your life. Are they true? Do they lift you up or tear you down? If they empower you to focus on the good, like the second brother did, focus on them. If they do not do that, as was the case for the first brother, then discard them.

You can choose your reaction to your circumstances. That is just a fact!

> **WISDOM NUGGET #6:** The problem is not the problem. Your attitude towards the problem is the problem.

Discussion questions on Blog No. 3:

1. Do you sometimes let the momentum of your thoughts make a situation appear much worse than it actually is?
2. Does changing the way you look at things as a mindset make sense to you, or are you skeptical of that?
3. Which of the two brothers in the scenario talked about in this blog most resemble the way you generally look at things?

BLOG NO. 4: Self-Care Comes First

One thing most of us have been told since we were little children is: Don't be selfish!

Our parents (if they were good parents), encouraged us to help other people, share our toys, and consider the needs of other people. That is great advice, as being generous and caring towards other people is truly an empowering way for all of us to live.

But have some of us perhaps taken that sentiment too far? Have we become so fixated at looking after the people in our lives first that we've forgotten about our own needs?

Blog No. 4 discusses that, and uses the classic example of the airline industry. Anybody who has ever been on an airplane knows that you are told to put your own mask on first in the event of an emergency, even before helping small children and people with disabilities.

Is that not selfish behavior? Or is it just logical and responsible behavior? Read this blog and then consider the questions at the end to answer that question with your mentor.

Airlines have it right - put your own face mask on first

In preparation for take-off, every airline flight reviews the safety procedures the plane has. And on every flight the crew says the same thing about what you should do if the air mask bags should deploy at any time.

Put your own mask on first, you are told, even before assisting small children and disabled people. We've all heard that every time we've flown, because every flight attendant has the same message, regardless of the airline.

Put your own mask on first.

It makes perfect sense of course. Even though the first inclination would be for us to help others with their masks beforehand (especially small children or people who need assistance), the reality is that once we have ours in place and fully functioning, we will then be in a better position to help others.

Help yourself first - then turn your attention to helping others. That is the clear message being sent on every flight that you will ever take.

That is a great way for airlines to operate, and it's a great way for all of us to operate as well…in the air, or on the ground!

Being a selfless person is a noble trait. Putting the needs of others ahead of your needs is commendable to be sure. What you give you get after all, so showing kindness and compassion to others is a sure sign that when you need kindness and compassion in return, it will come to you.

We got that. But the person who most needs to be loved and looked after by you is – YOU. And that is not selfish. That is self-love, and it is something that all of us need to do for OURSELVES.

Most of us hope to be able to positively impact the lives of other people in some way. Most human beings, when you dig deep down, are caring and want to help others. Some people make that their priority, even over their own needs.

That's very selfless. That's very noble. It's also not necessary - and also not advisable in most cases.

Our greatest opportunity to positively affect someone else's life is to start positively working on our own. Do you want to be someone who gives money to charity for instance? Well you can't give what you don't have. People who are broke can't help people who need money. They don't have any to give.

Do you want to teach someone an important skill or trait that can make their lives better? Well you can't teach what you don't know. A great teacher in any walk of life has to first learn and understand the material fully before they can successfully pass it on to someone else. It takes years of learning – it takes decades usually in fact – to be a qualified teacher in any field. You can't teach somebody else a skill you don't already have.

We all want love. It's the human universal need. But until we learn to really love ourselves, the love we give to others will never really be complete. Parents are always trying to make their children feel good about themselves and love them unconditionally – but how can that be passed on to any child by someone who deep down doesn't feel that way about themselves? The best learning tool any parent can give to a child is a good example.

If you want to be a great philanthropist, then go out and make a lot of money and then give it away if you must! If you want to be a great teacher or mentor, get the formal education or life experience first then pass that on to someone who yearns to be taught what you already know. If you want to spread your love around please do, the world is crying for that – but make sure you start at home. Start with yourself.

Treat yourself like you would treat your best friend. Talk to yourself that way too. The more happy, successful, smart and rich you become, the more you will be able to give to others.

Self-love is not narcissism, because you deserve to give yourself the best before you give the world your best.

Put your own mask on first.

WISDOM NUGGET #7: The airlines are right –
put your own face mask on first.

Discussion questions on Blog No. 4:

1. Did your parents constantly preach to you that you should not be selfish, even to the point of you going without something so somebody else could have it?
2. Talk with your mentor about how you feel about this issue – do you consider yourself more of a selfish person or a selfless person?
3. How does the thought of looking after yourself first and foremost make you feel?

BLOG NO. 5: Start The Day Right

Many of us can only wish that we had the dedication and discipline that the famed Navy Seals have.

A Navy Seal's life is not for the meek. They have incredibly high standards to maintain. The grueling training they have to endure just to become a Navy Seal – not to mention how they have to live after they pass the training – makes Navy Seals a very rare breed indeed. Out of the thousands that try to become a Seal, only a handful can make it through the training.

Blog No. 5 looks at what makes the Navy Seals so great. It is their attention to detail, it is the way they look after the little things in a big way (because there actually aren't any little things), and it's the way they start their day and set the tone for a successful one.

It all starts by making their bed – perfectly!

While only a very small percentage of people will ever become Navy Seals, or even want to become Navy Seals, is there something we can all learn from them that we can adapt in our own lives? Read this blog and then consider the points below to explore the answer to that question.

Be a Navy Seal – start your day by making your bed!

There are few people on earth tougher and more disciplined than the famous Navy Seals.

The training someone has to endure to become a Navy Seal is infamous and legendary. Only a few can survive the grueling weeks of incredibly demanding physical and mental torment that is required to graduate as a Navy Seal.

It has brought some of the toughest and strongest people in America to their knees. Most candidates who start the regime quit, as usually no more than 25 percent of those selected to even attempt the program manage to complete it.

Every day starts the same during this training for these remarkable candidates. It's an early rise, and the first task they have is to make their bed.

But they do not just slop the sheets down and be done with it of course – they must "Make Your Bed." It has to be perfect. The test comes when the instructors bounce a quarter off the blankets and the quarter bounces right back up into their hands; that's how tightly the sheets must be in place.

Navy Seals are the elite of the elite of the United States military. They must be incredibly fit. Once selected, they become the people who accept and tackle the most dangerous missions, the missions that require the most of a person's mental and physical capabilities. Their training days are incredibly long and filled with mind boggling brutal training sessions, from sunrise to sunset.

So…what possible reason is there for them being so particular about how they make their bed during training?

It's because that's how they start their day. It's their beginning. It sets the tone. And for a Navy Seal, that is the reason why making their beds so well is so important.

Admiral William H. McRaven wrote a great book several years ago that became a No. 1 bestseller. It's called "Make Your Bed. Little Things That Can Change Your Life…And Maybe The World."

Admiral McRaven gave the commencement speech at the University of Texas, a speech that went viral. Here's some of what he said in that speech to the graduating class on why THEY should make their beds:

"If you make your bed every morning, you will have accomplished the first task of the day. It will give you a small sense of pride and it will encourage you to do another task and another and another. By the end of the day, that one task completed will have turned into many tasks completed. Making your bed will also reinforce the fact that the little things in life matter. If you can't do the little things right, you will never do the big things right."

We are not Navy Seals. But we can learn a lot from them on how they start their day, and the approach they take to doing the little things right before they take on the big things.

Starting your day off by making your bed gives you a sense of structure. It sets the tone. It gives you a feeling of accomplishment. When you do it perfectly, you get a sense of pride. It provides some motivation to do the other tasks ahead of you today as well as you can.

After they make their beds, the day of a Navy Seals candidate is incredibly demanding. It's filled with punishing training and dangerous assignments. They press their bodies to the absolute limit, and are challenged both physically and mentally beyond belief.

Our days aren't nearly as tough (be honest – they aren't!). But many of us face long and demanding days ahead in our own right, filled with challenges we have to face and tasks that we need to accomplish. How do we best prepare for those long and challenging days?

Start them off right. Do the little things well. Do the things you need to do with a sense of pride. Create some momentum for the day by doing a task well and then following up that next task with another one, and another one, and another one.

Before you know it – you are rolling! Action creates momentum, not the other way around. Get up, stretch, and face the new day with a smile on your face and a sense of gratitude. It's a fresh 24 hours to do the little things right, and then do the big things right.

You either run the day, or the day runs you. That's why the Navy Seals know it's important to start the day right. You can do that too.

Make Your Bed!

> **WISDOM NUGGET #8:** Instead of asking what you can get out of life, ask what you can give to it.

Discussion questions on Blog No. 5:

1. Navy Seals feel that the way you start your day working on the smallest task can create momentum that you can build on for the rest of the day. Do you agree?
2. Navy Seals feel that by doing the little things right, you can more easily do the big things right. Do you agree with that line of thinking?
3. Do you make your bed in the morning?

BLOG NO. 6: Balance Yourself All Over

One of the most overused clichés of life is the struggle of having "work/life balance." Isn't that right?

What exactly does that even mean? Many of our clients wrestle with this dilemma all the time. They think that if they want to be successful, they have to give up other things in their lives that they like to do. It's just the price you have to pay, argue some of them.

Blog No. 6 addresses this issue and asks a question we asked in our blog regarding feelings: "Is that true?"

Do you really have to pay a significant price if you want to have great success? Is it not possible to have "balance" in your life if you want to be an ultra-achiever?

Before you even get into that answer, we believe that you first need to define what success means to you. And as you can see by reading this blog, first defining what success means to you will make the answer to what work/life balance really is clearer to you. Discuss your thoughts on this blog and review the questions with your PDC – we feel this topic is an especially important one.

Success means having a balanced life in all areas of it

It is perhaps the biggest challenge we all face in our lives – how do we achieve more success and still have some balance?

Does great success in our careers always have to come with great sacrifice in our personal life? Where is the happy medium for those of us who want more from our careers, but still want to enjoy our family, friends, hobbies, etc.? Is it really a case of "either/or" when it comes to having huge career achievements?

It can be very difficult to find balance in life. On one hand the world is saying that you have to dedicate thousands and thousands of hours to your craft to become great (the 10,000 hour rule); on the other hand the world is also saying nobody ever died wishing they had spent more time at the office. No wonder we make ourselves miserable sometimes by just thinking about this core life issue!

It's not easy finding balance, but here are three steps to follow.

1. **Stop listening to the world**. Listen to your heart instead. Everybody's definition of success is different. We all want more out of life but everybody's definition of "more" is different. We sometimes create stress just thinking about the stress we are under to try and do everything. Stop. Breathe. Ask yourself what is most important to YOU - not what you think is most important to the world. Once you answer that question honestly, it's easier to live your values. Not everyone wants or needs to be a billionaire – really! And not everyone finds the thought of working 80 hours a week awful either. Really!

2. **Have a vision for your life.** Many of us spend more time planning our vacations than we do our careers. The biggest reason people don't have what they want in life is that they don't know what they want. Once you visualize what an ideal life looks like for you, it will be easier to prioritize what matters the most. Everybody should have a "To Do List" but that list should be prioritized by

the most important items first, not just random things to do. Tie them to your vision and watch how much easier life gets for you.

3. **Practice mindfulness.** When you are here, be here. Living in the moment helps you really absorb the work you need to do, and really helps you enjoy your leisure to the fullest. Multi-tasking is passé – the best way to get things done is to fully concentrate on one thing at a time. For example, if you can only manage to play with your kids for an hour today because work is calling, then make the absolute best of that hour. Don't live yesterday, today and tomorrow at the same time. A full hour of total engagement with your family is better than two hours of being distracted and on your phone while you are with them.

There is a great parable of a rich old American tourist who is visiting Mexico and on a boat. He is enjoying his time and sees a young local man working hard to make the tourists happy.

He calls the young man over and asks him what he does.

"I work on the boat all day, from 9 to 5," he says. "I am an employee, been here for several years."

The rich tourist then asks him what he does after 5.

"Most days I have dinner and then go to the beach and hang around to play my guitar with my friends."

The rich tourist shakes his head. "Young man, you can do better than that. You should get here even earlier, work later, and one day, you won't just work on the boat you will own the boat! And if you work really hard, you can own several boats! Then you will be rich like me and be successful, not just a worker!"

The young man considers this and looks at the rich old tourist. "Then what will I do?" he asks.

The rich old tourist gets impatient and yells "Well then you can go hang around on the beach and play your guitar with your friends!"

What do you want in life friends? Live your values, not the values of a rich old tourist, or a young worker who doesn't want to be an owner, or anyone else. Do what is important to YOU. Everyone's definition of success is different. Develop a clear vision for what you want and a plan to accomplish it - then live your life accordingly.

When you do that, you'll find it is much easier to achieve balance between work and play. Then by all means go out and work hard and play hard – and live in the moment. We only have moments to live after all!

> ## WISDOM NUGGET #9: A convenient time doesn't just come to you, you choose it.

Discussion questions on Blog No. 6:
1. Do you have a clear idea of how you want your ideal life to look like? Is your vision easy for you to articulate?
2. Did reading this blog make you feel uncomfortable about how you are currently living on a day-to-day basis?
3. Are you living the kind of life you really want to live, or are you living the way you think the world wants you to live? Be honest here, this is an important thing to discover as you examine your life's journey.

BLOG NO. 7: Failure Is Good For You

Most of us realize that of all the things that stop us from achieving our goals, likely the biggest one is fear.

Our fears really hamper our progress. One of the biggest fears that stop many of our clients from crafting the kind of life they want is their fear of failure. For some that fear of failure is so strong, they don't even attempt the things they want to do in the first place.

Why don't many people even try to start a new business, or leave a job they don't like, or set out to start a new relationship with someone? Because they are afraid they are going to fail. Hey, who likes losing out, right?

Blog No. 7 talks about failure and how we often fear it. But it shows us that we don't succeed despite our failures, we succeed because of them.

When you have the right attitude you never lose when you try something - you either win or learn.

Read this blog and see if the questions below make you ask yourself if you have any fears that are stopping you from achieving the kind of success that you want.

We don't succeed despite failure, we succeed because of failure!

Fear stops us from doing a lot of things, and there are a lot of fears that are responsible for that. The biggest one is the fear of failure.

Who wants to fail after all? The word itself is scary – FAILURE. It's depressing just to look at it, especially in all caps!

But not only should we not fear failure, we should embrace it. The only people who never fail at anything, of course, are those who never try any-thing. We don't enjoy great success at anything in life without having to deal with failures from time to time, and we all know that.

Sure we do. However – like anything that we know that is worth knowing, we need to be reminded of it. And in the case of failure, we need to be reminded that we have to accept it and deal with it happening; but we also have to be told that we should EMBRACE failure.

That's right, embrace it. Not just tolerate it, not just accept it, but embrace it.

We learn more from failure than we do from success, if we look at it the right way. And sometimes our greatest successes come directly as a result of our "failures" which in retrospect aren't failures at all.

The Rocket Chemical Company is a perfect example of that. In 1953, the company was set up to create a water displacement formula to be used as a rust-prevention solvent and degreaser in the aerospace industry.

They failed to do it on the first attempt. And they failed again on another 38 attempts as well. All in all – 39 failures! Until finally, on the 40th attempt, they found success – success that would not have been possible without the lessons learned from the previous 39 failures.

By the way - that product is known worldwide as WD-40. Its name comes from "Water Displacement perfected on the 40th try." By 2015 the company had a $1.3 billion valuation and the product has more than 2,000 uses. That's quite the failure!

The 3M Company is another example. In 1968, their engineers were attempting to come up with an ultra-strong adhesive for use in aircraft construction. Instead, a mistake led to a new adhesive called acrylate co-polymer microspheres, which was a weak, pressure-sensitive adhesive. It was a complete failure – although the developed product did have a sticking tangent it was far too weak, which meant that the sticky substance could be peeled away without leaving residue and reused. It was an interesting development for a product, but it made it totally useless for using in an aircraft.

For 10 years the product either laid doormat, or potential uses for it failed in the marketplace. Until 1978 that is, when another attempt was made to test its marketability. Finally – success!

And the Post-It note was born. Ever hear of it?!

The same rule of failure being beneficial in the development of products applies to individuals. We are all familiar with the great success stories of athletes, actors and world leaders who thrived after numerous failures. This is one of our favorites – check out this person's litany of failure:

- 1816: His family was forced out of their home. He had to work to support them.
- 1818: His mother died.
- 1831: Failed in business.
- 1832: Ran for state legislature – lost.
- 1832: Also lost his job that year – wanted to go to law school but couldn't get in.
- 1833: Borrowed some money from a friend to begin a business and by the end of the year he was bankrupt. He spent the next 17 years of his life paying off this debt.
- 1834: Ran for state legislature again – won.

- 1835: Was engaged to be married, sweetheart died and his heart was broken.
- 1836: Had a total nervous breakdown and was in bed for six months.
- 1838: Sought to become speaker of the state legislature – defeated.
- 1840: Sought to become elector – defeated.
- 1843: Ran for Congress – lost.
- 1846: Ran for Congress again – this time he won – went to Washington, D.C. and did a good job.
- 1848: Ran for re-election to Congress – lost.
- 1849: Sought the job of land officer in his home state – rejected.
- 1854: Ran for Senate of the United States – lost.
- 1856: Sought the Vice-Presidential nomination at his party's national convention – got less than 100 votes.
- 1858: Ran for U.S. Senate again – again he lost.

My heavens that's more than enough failure for one person to endure in a lifetime! Oh, but we forgot the final line of his bio:

- 1860: Elected President of The United States

Not only was Abraham Lincoln "Honest Abe" – he was Persistent Abe too!

Have you had failure in your life? Congratulations! That means you were out in the world trying to succeed. When at first you don't succeed – you are in some pretty good company. Do not fear failure. Do not just accept it and tolerate it. EMBRACE it. Learn from it.

That failure just might turn out to be the best thing that could have happened to you.

> ### WISDOM NUGGET #10: The grass isn't greener on the other side, its greener where you water it.

Discussion questions on Blog No. 7:

1. Given the number of times he failed, would you describe Abraham Lincoln as a failure in life? Did his failures actually help him become President?

2. Think about a time you suffered a failure either in your own business or personal life. Reflect on what you learned from the experience.

3. What fears do you think are holding you back from attempting something new? Is it the fear of failure - or perhaps it's the fear of success and all that comes with it that is your biggest fear?

BLOG NO. 8: It Is All About The Process

Clichés become clichés because they are said all the time – and because most times they are true. Case in point: "It's all about the process."

One of our all-time favorite quotes we used in one of our tweets was from the great tennis champion Martina Navratilova. She was the ultimate competitor and one of the most successful tennis players in the history of the sport.

She said: "The moment of victory is far too short to live for that and nothing else."

That is really just another way of saying it's all about the process. She really wanted to win every match and tournament and she celebrated all of her wins with the best of them. But if that was the only reason to play, she never would have lasted as long as she did, playing highly competitive tennis into her 50s.

Read Blog No. 8. Then when you talk to your PDC, discuss whether you think your moments of victory actually out-weighed the process it took to make them happen.

It really is all about the process

You hear it all the time...stay focused on the process and stay detached from the results.

It makes sense when you think about it, right? Once you've done the hard work and put in the time on planning and preparing, the best thing to do next is not get caught up in the results. If you are doing things the right way the wins will come eventually...is how the mantra goes.

Or as the great John Wooden, legendary coach of UCLA's men's basketball team put it: "The score will take care of itself when you take care of the effort that precedes the score."

That's simple right? Sure seems to be. But is it easy to actually do that? Simple things are sometimes not that easy to do.

When you focus on the results over the process, you can get into trouble. Many sports fans think that when a team loses a game horribly, the coach will get mad and yell at his players. But ask many veteran coaches and they'll tell you that they don't have to yell at their players after a bad loss – they know they stunk!

Good coaches get angry with their teams when they play poorly but somehow fluke out a win on a lucky break, and laugh about it afterwards. Sometimes teams prepare poorly and play poorly, yet still manage to get a positive result. It happens.

And sometimes you can do all the right things, prepare well and play well, and a bad bounce or an injury or a bad officiating call can leave you with a negative result. That happens too.

In the long run however, the team that "takes care of the effort" will win far more often than the team that is just fixated on the results. It really is all about the process. Nobody can get lucky and stay lucky enough to be a long-term winner without doing all of the work that needs to be done before the results are even known.

There is another important reason to detach yourself from the results of your efforts. Once the work has been done, being fixated on the result is just another form of worry – the most useless emotion of all.

Say you get an interview for a job you badly want. You spend hours and hours researching the company, put together a presentation for them, and then dress sharp and go in and give a great interview. Well done!

But then comes the waiting. That can be hard. But there is no point in becoming fixated on the result of this one job interview. You have "taken care of the effort" so the best thing to do is to move on to something else until the verdict is in. If you do get the job, that's great. If not, you'll get one eventually thanks to your work ethic.

The incomparable Zig Ziglar, one of the best motivational speakers of all time, compared it to what a pro bowler does. The bowler grabs the ball, stares down the alley at the pins, positions the ball so he's comfortable, and rolls it down the lane. If the bowler has practiced hard, and worked on the form over and over, chances are he will have good results on that shot and for the entire game. Those that haven't practiced will likely have poor results, although even the worst bowler from time to time manages a strike or two. The law of averages catches up to everybody.

But have you seen the way some amateur bowlers try to "encourage" the ball?! They yell at it, they wave their arms in the air to try and guide the ball, and jump up and down pleading for a strike. What good does that do? They may as well just turn around and get another ball because the result is out of their hands as soon as the ball leaves their hands!

Sometimes in life, the result of what we want is indeed out of our hands. We've done the work, we've tossed the ball and the result will be whatever it is. Worrying about where the ball is going to go after you've released it is pointless.

If you have done the planning and preparation and your effort was there, whether that one throw glides perfectly down the middle or not shouldn't discourage you. And if you haven't practiced or planned or done the work, a lucky strike, or a team win, or even getting a job (perhaps because there were no other candidates), should not be a cause for celebration. If you try and "cheat" on the effort, it will catch up to you at some point. It always does.

It takes a combination of hard work, talent and a little luck to succeed in sports or in business. But here's the thing that Coach Wooden knew – the hard working, talented people seem to get all the luck too!

Do the work. Focus on the process. The results will take care of themselves. And if you take care of the effort and stay true to the process, you'll win far more times than you lose.

> WISDOM NUGGET #11: What you become
> as a result of chasing your goals
> is more important than reaching them.

Discussion questions on Blog No. 8:

1. Do you have trouble detaching yourself from the results of your work when it's all done and you are just waiting for the result?
2. Do you think luck plays far too much a role in the success most people attain in life, or is luck just preparation meeting opportunity?
3. Ask yourself this honest question – are your efforts most of the time good enough so that if you don't get what you're after, you can still feel good about the process?

BLOG NO. 9: Quantity Over Quality

It's not how many things you do that matters, it's the quality of the things that you do that's important. Its quality over quantity, we've all heard that a million times.

And for the most part I am sure we can all agree on that being the truth. But is that ALWAYS the case?

One thing Jim, Chris and Roger all have in common is a heavy involvement in sports. Jim was an owner; Chris was a General Manager/Coach and Roger a broadcaster/executive. So Blog No. 9 uses successful sports athletes as examples of where in some cases, quantity can really help us get to where we want to go.

The late Kobe Bryant of the Los Angeles Lakers and Alex Ovechkin of the Washington Capitals are the best two examples of superstar athletes who have been of the highest quality – but are also known for taking the most shots. They were always among the top scoring leaders but also always at the top of the missed shots category.

It's a simple philosophy when you think of it – the more hooks you have in the lake, the better chances you have of catching a fish. Read Blog No. 9

and ask yourself if you shouldn't be taking more shots at success, instead of always waiting for just the right moment. Ask your PDC if he thinks quantity can sometimes make a difference in your fishing for success!

If you want to score more goals take more shots

"If you want to catch more fish, use more hooks." – George Allen

Quality over quantity...isn't that always right?

We hear that all the time. It is one of the cornerstones of success in life and in business. The number of things you produce isn't what's important, it's the quality of what you are producing that counts.

That makes perfect sense. We all admire quality more than just quantity. And even though anything of quality generally takes longer and is more expensive to produce as a result, most people want quality items not fast and cheap ones.

That is true of products and of services too. Whatever business or walk of life you are in, the best way to go is always ensure quality over quantity. It doesn't matter how many, what really matters is how good.

So it is always quality over quantity for true success right?

Right – but let's not dismiss the value of quantity either.

Do you know who the all-time leader in missed shots in the history of the NBA is? It's not even close. He had a stunning 14,481 missed field goals. That's over 1,000 more missed shots than the guy who is in second place. My goodness!

The answer is the late Kobe Bryant.

Bryant was one of the greatest NBA players ever. He ranks third all-time in points scored and is a legend in Los Angeles Lakers history.

He trails only Kareem Abdul-Jabbar and Karl Malone in career points scored. Abdul-Jabbar is sixth all-time in misses; Malone ranks fourth. Also among those in the top 10 in career misses are Michael Jordan and LeBron James. Of the top 30 on the missed shots list, all of them are either in the Hall of Fame or will be soon.

Wayne Gretzky is the NHL's all-time goals leader with 894. On the career shooting percentage list, The Great One ranks 43rd. Top three in shooting success are Craig Simpson, Charlie Simmer and Paul MacLean – really good NHL players, but they don't get called "The Great One" like No. 99 does.

"You miss 100% of the shots you don't take." – Wayne Gretzky

Alex Ovechkin has a crack at beating Gretzky's goals record in the next few years perhaps. Wouldn't that be amazing? But do you know where he ranks on the list of top shooting percentage in NHL history?

I don't know either. The published list only covers the top 250. Ovechkin's career shooting percentage isn't even among the top several hundred of all-time. So how did he get to within shouting distance of Gretzky's career goals record?

He took a lot of shots!

Who is the all-time walks leader among Major League Baseball pitchers? Again, no contest – the leader has 2,795. Nobody else has ever walked over 2,000 batters in a career for heaven's sake. Who could that be?

Nolan Ryan. By the way, he's also the career strikeouts leader with 5,714. Nobody else has ever hit the 5,000 mark.

Who as the most losses for a pitcher all-time in baseball? This guy has 315 career losses. My God that's horrible! That's 20 losses a year for more than 15 years, who did that?

Cy Young. He's also first all-time in career wins with 511. And the best pitcher award in baseball is named after him.

I could go on here, but you get the point I'm sure. What Kobe Bryant, Wayne Gretzky, Alex Ovechkin, Nolan Ryan and Cy Young all have in common is greatness in their sport. What they also have in common in addition to their quality was their quantity.

Gretzky is the 43rd most accurate shooter of all-time. Ovechkin is even further down that list. But as Gretzky famously said, you miss 100 percent of the shots you don't take.

Whatever you are trying to accomplish in your life, whether it's personal or business, you should always strive for quality. Produce the best work you can, have high standards, and give the world you're best. You – and the world – deserve that.

But if you really want to be considered one of the all-time greats in your field, remember the lesson of Bryant, Gretzky, Ovechkin, Ryan and Young too. They are considered legends because they weren't afraid to shoot either – or walk a guy – or lose a lot of games.

If you want to make more sales, make more calls. If you want to have more "hits" in life, make more losses. If you want to catch more fish, use more hooks.

Quality is what really matters, but quantity can lead to great things for you as well. Keep swinging. Don't be afraid to miss. Don't be afraid to lose so you can win.

After all – even though four quarters are a lot easier to carry around than 100 pennies - if you need one dollar both of them still add up to a buck!

> **WISDOM NUGGET #12: A 1% improvement a day over a year is a 365% improvement.**

Discussion questions on Blog No. 9:

1. Many sales managers insist their staff make a certain number of calls a day, regardless of how efficient those calls may turn out to be. Do you agree with this strategy?

2. Do you sometimes find yourself the victim of "paralysis by analysis" when it comes time to making a decision? Are you sometimes afraid to shoot?

3. Did reading this blog change your thinking a bit about not always waiting for the perfect time to take a shot, as 100% of the shots you don't take…?

BLOG NO. 10: Change The Forecast

We all want to know what the weather forecast is, especially if our plans for that day – or that week, or month – involve a lot of outdoor time.

Quite often we're disappointed to hear that the forecast calls for rain, and that could ruin our plans. But we are really disappointed when the forecast says sunny and it rains anyway, so the forecast turns out being wrong.

There is nothing we can do about the weather forecast. But as Blog No. 10 tells us, it's based on a key element – what current patterns are showing. If a storm is headed our way for instance, the forecast is made under the assumption current conditions will remain the same and the storm will not "blow off" because of changing patterns.

"If current trends continue" is common weather parlance. The forecast will be accurate if the trends do continue, and not accurate (for either good or bad) if they don't. Blog No. 10 reminds us that we too make our own forecasts.

However unlike the meteorologists, we can change those current conditions whenever we want to. We can change those patterns. We can change our personal long range forecasts. When you finish reading, see if the questions get you thinking about how to change yours.

You can't change the weather forecast but you can change your own

Everybody checks the weather forecast. We all want to know what the weather is going to be.

We're planning a trip, so we need to know the forecast. We have outdoor plans, so we want to know the chance of rain. We have to drive a long way, so before we set out we want to know the weather conditions.

Weather forecasting is pretty important therefore. But how accurate is the weather forecast? For the most part weather forecasts are accurate, but often enough they turn out to be wrong.

There is a simple reason that the weather forecast misses (especially the longer away it is; the daily forecast and the long-range accuracy forecast accuracy are wildly different). That reason is this – it is based on what conditions look like today.

"We're tracking this storm and will keep you updated," the forecasters tell us. "Current trends show we could be in for a storm in the next 48-72 hours."

But even with all the technology they have, often the forecast is "wrong" and the storm doesn't come. Why is that?

It is because conditions have changed. The weather patterns of Monday are often not the same as the ones on Wednesday. So the weather forecaster wasn't wrong to say on Monday a storm was coming on Wednesday, because on Monday the conditions were in place for a storm - but those trends changed. All weather forecasts are based on current patterns and current conditions. A lot can change in a few days with the weather though.

The same thing can be true for you if you feel you are trending in the wrong direction. A lot can change in your personal forecast too, and sometimes quickly. Perhaps you think a storm is brewing for you.

You are quite possibly right. As you sit here today, you may be thinking you are in for a financial crisis in the next few months. You may feel stuck at your job and thinking you'll have to quit soon. Your health might be poor and you are on track for some serious issues.

You may be right. That could be an accurate forecast – based on today's conditions. But here's the key to when you think like this – even if your forecast is right, it is only based on current trends...current tracking... current conditions.

We can't do anything about the weather conditions. We're stuck with the weather. But we can change the conditions that are causing us to have our own gloomy life forecast.

Are you in a financial pinch because you overspent? Then your forecast might show financial storm clouds on the way soon. Is your health getting bad because of bad lifestyle habits? Then your forecast might be a trip to the hospital soon. Doing a lousy job at work because you think you're stuck there? Then your forecast might be unemployment coming for you around the corner.

You may be trending that way today. Current conditions might indicate that if patterns remain the same, that could be the 7-day forecast for you. It could be the longer term forecast for you too.

But it doesn't have to be. Some of our clients think their personal forecast is out of their control, just like the weather forecast is. It's not.

"Change is never painful, only the resistance to change is painful." – Buddha

Deal with your financial issues head on. Draw up a personal budget. Get some help if you need it. Come to grips with it and work hard at managing your money better.

Get off the couch and get moving. Start an exercise program and begin eating better. Look after yourself, and that includes your mental health as well. Don't just sit there letting bad health and bad thoughts continue.

If you can't tolerate your job, find another one. If that's not feasible, then make the best of the job you have. Either quit the job or do the job better, but either way don't bitch about it. Focus on solutions to your problems, not on the problems themselves.

Maybe your personal forecast is trending towards some stormy times. Maybe it looks a little bleak. But that is based on current patterns that you can change with the right attitude. The best way to create a better future is with a better present.

"It doesn't matter where you are you are nowhere compared to where you can go." – Bob Proctor.

An old adage is: "If you don't like the weather right now stick around. It'll change." That's very true. Weather patterns and circumstances change all the time; nothing we can do about that other than wait for the changes.

But with our own personal forecast? It's based on our current behavior patterns, and those we can change and control.

Don't like your forecast? Get busy changing the conditions. If you do your long range forecast will turn out a lot better.

WISDOM NUGGET #13: Accept your present reality, but not its permanence.

Discussion questions on Blog No. 10:
1. Life can be a self-fulfilling prophecy. Under current conditions, do you think your long-term forecast is a good one?
2. What are some of the things you are doing right now that are hurting your chances of making your dreams a reality? What are some of the things you are doing that are helping?
3. Do you think habits are easy to change? Are old thinking patterns easy to change?

SUMMARY OF BLOGS

There are many different approaches you can take to make your life more successful. Sometimes we find ourselves simply overwhelmed with all of the choices we face, and many of our clients have admitted to us that they just don't know where to start.

Our advice is consistent on this one: just start somewhere. Open up your mind to all the possibilities that are out there to make yourself be better. Hopefully reading these blogs and discussing the questions with your PDC helps you unlock some of the barriers that may be holding you back from living your best life.

There is no "one size fits all" approach to making a breakthrough in your life. It comes from being relentless in your pursuit of creating a better mindset, and that comes from spending some time reading and studying the best ways for you to accomplish that.

Next up for our TEAMMATES clients: the audio component of our program. Please get that and listen to it all. Have a pen and paper with you to make notes on the issues discussed throughout the shows you'll be listening to. Jim, Chris or Roger will discuss them with you during your individual sessions.

If you aren't in our program, please continue reading. Let's move over to our daily inspirations. Because as you run through all of this material, a little extra blast of motivation might be in order to keep you inspired!

DAILY INSPIRATIONS

Since we officially started TEAMMATES in June 2019, we have been posting daily tweets and Facebook updates on our Twitter and Facebook accounts. Why? Because we believe the world needs daily inspiration… and so do you.

In the Introduction Roger talked about the plethora of self-help books that are on the market. The same can be said for the large number of Twitter accounts and Facebook posts that use motivational quotes to keep us all inspired.

We at TEAMMATES believe that there can't be too many of these kinds of accounts. Social media is also filled with a lot of vitriol and hatred, so it is refreshing to see many individuals, organizations and companies taking the time to send an uplifting message on a regular basis. More power to them all for doing that.

We have been on board with that way of thinking since our inception – however we did have a strategy behind our messages.

First, we send out one message a day - just one. With all of the accounts out there, we just wanted to add our small part to the parade without overwhelming anybody. We stuck to just one that resonated with us.

Second, we also put our own spin on our daily quote. Many accounts send out just a famous quote or passage, while others send out an inspiring message written in their own words. We do both.

Over the years Roger has collected a lot of quotes and he has always used one in his final tweet on his Sportsnet 590 The Fan radio shows, just as a way of signing off. We used a lot of that collection, and then added our TEAMMATES message under it on a once-a-day basis.

Third, even though we personally selected the quote and wrote our own message under it, we didn't do this to promote our ventures. Our goal with these messages was not to promote TEAMMATES – we promote our business in other ways – but to add our input to the large number of tweeters and Facebook posters who think it's a good idea to send out a positive thought to the universe just because it's the right thing to do. Getting inspired is sometimes difficult and staying inspired is sometimes even more difficult.

We brought our entire first year's collection into this book for you to read and enjoy. Soak in the meaning of each of them and really pay attention to the message. When you are speaking with Jim, Roger or Chris, let us know which of these was especially meaningful to you. Do the same thing if you are doing these exercises with someone else.

It can be amazing how a positive message can be sent at just the right time somebody needs to hear it. Many times over the past few years we've received a note from someone saying that the message we sent was just the one they needed to hear right at that moment. We believe that is no coincidence.

As you can see while you take this course, our coaching methods are built on the foundation of positive thinking. We believe that we all need to build a solid foundation of principles we can draw on in good times and bad.

Our foundation pillars are gratitude, optimism and mindfulness. That's why we selected famous quotes that help spread those messages, and we took the time to add our thoughts on how the daily quote we selected can help make your day a little bit brighter.

We are very proud of this workbook, the audio component and the personal mentoring we offer, and glad you are taking the time over this 30-day program to focus and study on it. We hope those of you working with someone else are doing the same thing. The best books are the ones you live and not just read.

We all need reminders of what we already know every day. Information worth sharing is worth repeating – so that's why we will always continue to tweet and Facebook our daily messages. Here's a year's worth of them in one spot just for you…because even though you have taken the important step of committing to a dedicated life improvement course, you can always use some daily inspirations to help keep you motivated.

Please enjoy these and feel free to share them any way you wish, either on Twitter, Facebook or elsewhere.

> WISDOM NUGGET #14: Abundance is being satisfied with what you have while you envision what you want.

TEAMMATES DAILY MESSAGES

Jan. 1
"We will open the book. Its pages are blank. We are going to put words on them ourselves. The book is called Opportunity & its first chapter is New Year's Day." – Edith Lovejoy Pierce
New Year, New Chances; it's time to write about the best year of your life. Happy New Year!

Jan. 2
"Hope...Smiles from the threshold of the year to come...Whispering 'it will be happier'..." –Alfred Lord Tennyson
If you have hope in a happier life to come, then you have everything you need to create one. Make the New Year be your best year. Believe it and you'll see it!

Jan. 3
"We are what we think. All that we have arises with our thoughts. With our thoughts, we make the world." – Buddha
You are not responsible for every thought that you have, just for the ones that you dwell on. You become what you think, so focus on the thoughts that empower you!

Jan. 4

"Life is always walking up to us and saying 'Come on in, the living is fine.' And what do we do? Back off and take its picture."–
Russell Baker

Life is not meant to just be observed. It's meant to be lived. Get in the game. Stay active. Engage with life. The living is fine!

Jan. 5

"He who knows that enough is enough will always have enough." –
Lao Tzu

The world has enough for everyone's need but not enough for everyone's greed. If you aren't happy with what you have you won't be happy with what you get. Count your blessings. Be grateful!

Jan. 6

"Things turn out best for the people who make the best of the way things turn out." – John Wooden

There is some good in every bad thing that happens. There is something to be gained from every adversity. Make the best of your circumstances and your circumstances are better!

Jan. 7

"Change is never painful, only the resistance to change is painful."
– Buddha

Life changes all the time. We can fight change and be afraid of it, or we can embrace it and create a better life for ourselves. Choose the love of change over the fear of change!

Jan. 8

"If suffering continues, it's because we keep feeding our suffering."–
Thich Nhat Hanh

You emerge from dark times by looking for light, not by sitting in the dark. Look for the light to find your way out of the dark. If you stop feeding a stray cat it stops coming to your door!

Jan. 9
"How wonderful it is that nobody need wait a single moment before starting to improve the world."– Anne Frank
You don't have to wait a second to start living better. You can improve the world by improving yourself & making yourself a better person. And you can start right NOW!

Jan. 10
"A good traveler has no fixed plans and is not intent on arriving." – Lao Tzu
The journey is more important than the destination. The kind of person you become as a result of working on your goals is more important than achieving them. It really is all about the process!

Jan. 11
"Mistakes that are perceived as mistakes are often not mistakes at all." – Kirk Douglas
Don't beat yourself up over mistakes that you make. The only people that never make mistakes are those who do nothing of significance. And sometimes mistakes turn out to be the correct thing!

Jan. 12
"I am the master of my fate; I am the captain of my soul." – William Ernest Henley
You are in the driver's seat in your life. You are responsible for your decisions and thoughts. You control where your life goes. You aren't fearful of those facts, you are empowered by them!

Jan. 13
"Wanna fly; you gotta give up the shit that weighs you down." – Toni Morrison
Stop carrying the problems of the world around on your back. Many times it's just as important to let go as it is to hang on. When your past calls hang up on it. It has nothing new to say to you!

Jan. 14
"Never let your head hang down. Never give up and sit down and grieve. Find another way."– Satchel Paige
No matter what obstacles you face, stand up straight. Put your head up. Keep going. When you stand up to adversity, it shrinks before you. You are better than your problems!

Jan. 15
"A man is a success if he gets up in the morning and gets to bed at night, and in between he does what he wants to do."– Bob Dylan
Find something you are passionate about & spend as much time as you can doing it. There is no greater measure of success than doing what you love.

Jan. 16
"Some people think as soon as you plant a tree, it must bear fruit. We must allow it to grow a bit." – Tunku Abdul Rahman
Patience is not sitting around and just waiting. It is allowing the success seeds you've planted proper time to grow. Sometimes you just have to wait!

Jan. 17
"If you want to catch more fish, use more hooks." – George Allen
It's quality over quantity for sure. But if you want to hit more home runs, then step up to the plate more. The more you cast, the more you catch!

Jan. 18
"The cyclone derives its power from a calm center. So does a person." – Norman Vincent Peale
The calmer you can remain in a chaotic situation, the more likely it is you'll come out of it. Inner peace is not found outside of yourself; it comes from inside of you.

Jan. 19

"Nurture your mind with great thoughts, as you will never go higher than you think." – Benjamin Disraeli

Since we're all thinking anyways, why not think big? Have big dreams, big goals and big thoughts and you will do BIG things!

Jan. 20

"When we are no longer able to change a situation, we are challenged to change ourselves." – Viktor Frankl

There are some situations you can't change. But you can always change how you look at any situation. Don't try and change the world, just change the way you look at it.

Jan. 21

"If you remain calm in the midst of great chaos, it is the greatest guarantee that it will eventually subside." – Julie Andrews Edwards

Nothing in life is permanent, whether it is good or bad. This too shall pass. Draw on that thought to stay calm when bad weather arrives!

Jan. 22

"When written in Chinese, the word 'crisis' is composed of two characters. One represents danger and the other represents opportunity." – John F. Kennedy

In the very worst of situations there is some good. We become stronger as a result. We learn resiliency. This too shall pass!

Jan. 23

"We must be willing to get rid of the life we've planned, so as to have the life that is waiting for us." – Joseph Campbell

Planning is important but the plan isn't. Things are constantly changing. Be prepared to give up what you have planned for something that's even better!

Jan. 24
"There are more things that frighten us than injure us, and we suffer more in imagination than in reality." – Seneca
Many of your worries will never come to pass. The reality is worry is pointless and robs you of joy in the present moment. Imagine the possibilities instead!

Jan. 25
"The optimist sees opportunity in every danger the pessimist sees danger in every opportunity." – Winston Churchill
Optimists are realists too. They just choose to look for the good instead of the bad in their reality. Look for the good!

Jan. 26
"Life begins at the end of your comfort zone." – Neale Donald Walsh
There is only one way to get out of your comfort zone: Get out of your comfort zone! Everything you want in life is waiting for you on the other side of fear.

Jan. 27
"He who blames others has a long way to go on his journey. He who blames himself is half way there. He who blames no one has arrived." – Chinese proverb
Taking responsibility for your life isn't blaming yourself. It's empowering yourself to learn from life's lessons to be better!

Jan. 28
"Life isn't as serious as your mind makes it out to be." – Eckhart Tolle
Your mind sometimes spends a lot of time thinking everything is so serious. Not everything is. Laugh a little. Actually – laugh a lot! Enjoy your life!

Jan. 29

"Most of us spend too much time on what is urgent and not enough time on what is important." – Stephen Covey
Learning the difference between urgency and importance is vital for any business. It's vital for your happiness too. What's urgent usually isn't that important!

Jan. 30

"Failure is an attitude, not an outcome." – Harvey Mackay
If at first you don't succeed – well you are in pretty good company. You don't succeed despite your failures you succeed because of them. People who fail aren't failures!

Jan. 31

"Raise your words, not your voice. It is rain that grows flowers, not thunder." – Rumi
Yelling doesn't making you more right. It doesn't make more people listen to you. It's quality of words not the volume of your voice that matters. And remember that when you listen to others!

> WISDOM NUGGET #15: A rainstorm isn't a tornado.
> Don't make it one.

Feb. 1

"Experience is a hard teacher because she brings the test first, the lesson afterwards." – Vernon Law
It's hard to learn the hard way, but we all need to at times. Some experiences can be painful but the lessons are worth it with the right attitude. Win or learn!

Feb. 2

"Don't let the behavior of others affect your inner peace." — Dalai Lama

Your inner peace is yours. It does not belong to somebody else. So don't let anybody else take it from you. You can't control others, but you can control how you react to others.

Feb. 3

"Don't wait for the right opportunity. Create it." — George Bernard Shaw

You can't climb up the ladder of success with your hands in your pockets. Don't sit and wait for something to happen, go out and make something happen!

Feb. 4

"The most valuable player is the one who makes the most players valuable." — Peyton Manning

A great teammate is one who makes the other members of his team better. There is no "I" in "team" after all. Encourage the people around you & help make them better. That's a true MVP!

Feb. 5

"The primary cause of unhappiness is never the situation but your thoughts about it." — Eckhart Tolle

Is the situation you are facing really that bad? Or are you making it that bad by the way you are thinking about it? There is something good in even the worst situation.

Feb. 6

"One of the most tragic things I know about human nature is that all of us tend to put off living." — Dale Carnegie

What are you waiting for? Do you really want to do something? Then go do it. There is never a better time than NOW. Starting something creates momentum!

Feb. 7
"I've decided to be happy because it's good for my health."
— Voltaire
Circumstances don't make you happy or sad. What you think about them makes you happy or sad. The best way to stay healthy is to stay optimistic. There is some good in the worst of times. Attitude is a CHOICE!

Feb. 8
"Your worst enemy cannot harm you as much as your own unguarded thoughts." — Buddha
We get in our own way too often. We need to think about the way we are thinking. Practice mindfulness — you'll then be aware of how you are self-sabotaging yourself. Think like an optimist!

Feb. 9
"Spectacular achievements come from unspectacular preparation."
— Roger Staubach
There is no such thing as an overnight success. The hardest work gets done when nobody else is watching. When opportunity comes it is too late to prepare. Do your work now & you'll be ready!

Feb. 10
"If you are depressed, you are living in the past. If you are anxious, you are living in the future. If you are at peace, you are living in the present." — Lao Tzu
Don't live yesterday, today and tomorrow at the same time. You know which one to pick. We only have moments to live!

Feb. 11
"In the depths of winter I finally learned that within me there lay an invincible summer." —Albert Camus
Severe winter is always followed by spring. No storm lasts forever. And no matter what the conditions outside, inner peace is always available inside! Spring is coming!

Feb. 12

"What you think, you become. What you feel, you attract. What you imagine, you create." – Buddha

You are the author of your life. You are creating your life right now, for good and for bad. Think positive. Feel good. Imagine greatness. Go out and create a masterpiece!

Feb. 13

"Your life right now is a result of your dominant thoughts and daily actions." – Robin Sharma

What you focus on expands. If your dominant thoughts and actions are negative, that is what you'll get back. You can be positive about that! Positive thoughts lead to positive actions.

Feb. 14

"Things do not happen. They are made to happen." – John F. Kennedy

Don't wait for things to happen to you, go out and make them happen to you, and to the people you care about it. Take some positive action today!

Feb. 15

"Do what you have to do until you can do what you want to do." – Oprah Winfrey

The journey is the goal. The tough sledding is a part of it. The more you work through the tough spots, the more sweet spots you'll eventually have!

Feb. 16

"The most certain way to succeed is always to try just one more time." – Thomas Edison

You can bear trying something tough ONE more time right? Just one more time; we can do anything once. Just have that attitude every day and you're all set!

Feb. 17
"A critic is someone who knows the way but can't drive the car." – Kenneth Tynan
The worst player in the game is still better than any critic sitting and watching. Those that can't or won't do, criticize instead. Play the game of life yourself, don't analyze how others play!

Feb. 18
"You ought to be thankful a whole heaping lot for the people and places you're lucky you're not." – Dr. Seuss
The grass isn't always greener on the other side it is greener where you water it. Be grateful for where you are and who you are. Bloom where you're planted!

Feb. 19
"If you want to lift yourself up, lift up someone else." – Booker T. Washington
The best way to lift your mood is to lift the mood of someone else. Spread some joy even when you are lacking it yourself. You get back what you give; it will come back to you!

Feb. 20
"An unbending tree is easily broken." – Lao Tzu
Trees often bend a bit in stormy weather, but they rarely break. Surfers know how to handle the high waves; they don't conquer them, they just go with the flow! Ride out the storms when they come, none of them last forever.

Feb. 21
"The most important decision you make is to be in a good mood." – Voltaire
You don't have to change the world to be happier, you just have to change the way you look at it. Decide to look for the good not the bad. Change the way you look at things & the things you look at change!

Feb. 22

"There has never been a statue erected to honor a critic." — Zig Ziglar

Building a great life is sometimes hard. Criticizing the builders is always easy. If you want to leave a great legacy then be a builder, not a critic. Critics are a dime a dozen, builders are priceless!

Feb. 23

"Believe you can and you're halfway there." — Theodore Roosevelt

And sometimes you're more than halfway there just by believing. Have a vision for your life and focus on your big picture every day. Have faith in yourself. Go do the work. Believe it and you'll see it!

Feb. 24

"The score will take care of itself when you take care of the effort that precedes the score." — John Wooden

Do your work. Prepare. Don't sweat the results. If you consistently do the work and prepare, you'll get the results more often than not.

Feb. 25

"All things are difficult before they are easy." — Thomas Fuller

Watch a baby learn to walk. Watch someone first try to learn a computer. Things that are easy for you now were always hard when you first began. Life-long learning creates life-long success!

Feb. 26

"After all is said and done, more is said than done." — Aesop

Enough said...get doing!

Feb. 27

"Nothing will work unless you do." — John Wooden

Many people want a successful life, but won't do the work you need to do to make one. If you think nothing is working for you, maybe it's because you are the one not working!

Feb. 28

"You know how advice is - you only want it if it agrees with what you would do anyways." – John Steinbeck

We often think that honest feedback is "constructive" only when we agree with it. Accept the fact that just maybe, somebody knows more than you do. Learn from your mentors!

Feb. 29

"We don't stop playing because we grow old we grow old because we stop playing." – George Bernard Shaw

Never let the kid in you grow up. Children aren't the only ones who need playtime. Adults need to re-learn the value of playtime too. Work hard and play hard as well!

WISDOM NUGGET #16: The Winter Olympics are won in the summer.

Mar. 1

"If you could kick the person in the pants responsible for most of your trouble, you wouldn't stand for a month." – Theodore Roosevelt

Stop blaming the world for your troubles. The world has enough on its plate. Take responsibility for your troubles and go out and fix them!

Mar. 2

"You are today where your thoughts have brought you; you will be tomorrow where your thoughts take you." – James Allen

When you really come to understand the importance of examining your thoughts and focusing on the ones that can help you, you will be unstoppable!

Mar. 3
"Action speaks louder than words, but not nearly as often." –
Mark Twain
One lovely action is greater than the thousands of words you can use talking about the action you are going to take. Do more. Talk less!

Mar. 4
"I ask not blessings, but more wisdom, with which to make better use of the blessings I now possess." – Napoleon Hill
Take time to add up things in your life you would not take money for. Health. Family. Friends. Pets. Count the blessings you have. You are richer than you think!

Mar. 5
"If you wait, all that happens is that you get older." – Mario Andretti
There is no better time to do anything than right at this moment. Don't put off to the next moment what you can do in this moment. Grow where you're planted. Start somewhere. Do what you can while you can!

Mar. 6
"You'll never change your destination if you stop and throw stones at every dog that barks." – Winston Churchill
Ignore the noise. Stay on course. Let the critics talk while you perform!

Mar. 7
"Life is an ongoing process of choosing between safety (out of fear & a need for defense) & risk (for the sake of progress & growth). Make the growth choice a dozen times a day." – Abraham Maslow
Something not in your comfort zone - take a step outside it. That's how you grow!

Mar. 8

"Don't take tomorrow to bed with you." – Norman Vincent Peale
Your bed is not the place to review your day & plan for tomorrow. It's for sleeping. Review your day & plan for tomorrow first, then go to bed when you're sleepy. Have pleasant dreams!

Mar. 9

"If you are the smartest person in the room, then you are in the wrong room." – Confucius
You are the equal of the five people you spend the most time with. Imagine how much smarter you'd be if you spent the most time with four people smarter than you. You become the company you keep!

Mar. 10

"Quit feeling sorry for yourself." – Buck O'Neill
Self-esteem, self-love & self-confidence are such wonderful things we can give to ourselves. However there is nothing more demeaning we can give ourselves than the habit of self-pity. Be grateful for the good things in your life!

Mar. 11

"When what you are shouts so loudly in my ears, I cannot hear what you say." – Ralph Waldo Emerson
Actions are always louder than words, no matter how much the talker yells. Your legacy will come from what you do, not from what you say. Let your actions speak for you!

Mar. 12

"Preach the gospel at all times, but only use words when necessary."
– St. Francis of Assisi
Don't tell people what you are going to do, just do it. Set an example by your actions, not by your words. The world is improved by what you do, not by what you say.

Mar. 13

"Everybody wants to change the world, but nobody wants to change himself." – Leo Tolstoy

It's much easier to change one person than to try and change nearly 8 billion people. We can't control what the planet does, but we can control what we do. Be the change you seek!

Mar. 14

"None of us is as smart as all of us." – Ken Blanchard

A problem shared with one person is a problem halved. A problem shared with lots of people probably won't be a problem for long. All of us working together are better than one of us working alone. Get some teammates!

Mar. 15

"A man can fail many times, but he isn't a failure until he begins to blame somebody else." – John Burroughs

Blaming is a waste of time. Accept responsibility for your life, and you don't have to blame yourself either. Stop finding fault and start finding solutions instead!

Mar. 16

"Do the thing and you shall have the power." – Ralph Waldo Emerson

If you do what you are afraid to do, the power that fear has over you is gone. Take some action, any action, to do something about an issue that causes you fear. Living in faith & action, not fear, is empowering!

Mar. 17

"He who has a why to live for can bear with almost any how." – Fredrick Nietzsche

Ask yourself: 'What do I want in life?' Then ask the most important question: 'Why do I want it?' When you know why you really want something, you can put up with any of the hows to get it!

Mar. 18

"Social media promises an end to loneliness but basically produces an increase in solitude." – David Brooks, New York Times
Nothing is good or bad except in how it's used. Social media is a great tool or a waste of time.

Mar. 19

"What we want is not blind optimism but flexible optimism; optimism with its eyes open. We must be able to use pessimism's keen sense of reality when we need it, but without having to dwell in its dark shadows." – Martin Seligman
Optimism isn't blind it is seeing what's good!

Mar. 20

"It ain't what you don't know that gets you into trouble. It's what you know for sure that just ain't so." – Mark Twain
Question your beliefs. Are they outdated or just plain wrong? Are your beliefs about yourself & the world true? Be open to learning more. Be open to change.

Mar. 21

"Our chief want in life is somebody who will make us do what we can." – Ralph Waldo Emerson
The toughest coaches and teachers in our lives are often the ones who resonate with us the most. Good mentors get you to realize how great you can be if you put in the work!

Mar. 22

"Reality is created by the mind. We can change our reality by changing our mind." – Plato
There is no reality, there's only perception of it. The power of thoughts is enormous. Improve your mind, you improve your life. Change your mind. Reality is what you think it is!

Mar. 23
"When I let go of what I am, I become what I might be." – Lao Tzu
The first step on the path to improving your life is to realize you
don't want to stay where you are. It is never too late to start
becoming what you were meant to be. Let the past go and embrace
the new you.

Mar. 24
"Fear is that little dark room where negatives are developed." –
Michael Pritchard
Do what you fear and the fear dissolves. Fear knocked on the door.
Faith answered. There was nobody there!

Mar. 25
"A mentor is someone who allows you to see the hope inside
yourself." – Oprah Winfrey
Mentors don't tell you how to live, they help show you the potential
you already have inside to live better. Good mentors don't want you
to model them, they just want you to become a better you!

Mar. 26
"The more I practice, the luckier I get." – Arnold Palmer
It takes hard work, talent & some luck to really be successful. Funny
thing is hard working people become talented & they seem to get
all the luck! Luck is preparation meeting opportunity. Practice more,
get luckier!

Mar. 27
"Shallow men believe in luck and circumstance. Strong men believe
in cause and effect." – Ralph Waldo Emerson
Luck is when preparation meets opportunity. Do your work, be
prepared & when opportunity comes, you can take advantage. When
opportunity comes it is too late to prepare.

Mar. 28
"So many of our dreams at first seem impossible, then they seem improbable, and then, when we summon the will, they soon become inevitable."– Christopher Reeve
Get started. Keep going. Action creates momentum. And before you know it you are doing amazing things! Believe in YOU!

Mar. 29
"To be wronged is nothing unless you continue to remember it."
– Confucius
Bad things happen all the time. But when you continue to re-live past wrongs done to you, they happen to you more than once. Bad enough it happened, you don't have to let it happen again and again!

Mar. 30
"Don't set your mind on things you don't possess as if they were yours, but count the blessings you already possess."–
Marcus Aurelius
Being grateful is the key to being happy. If you aren't happy with what you have, you won't be happy with what you get. Always be grateful!

Mar. 31
"Continuous effort – not strength or intelligence – is the key to unlocking our potential." – Winston Churchill
Continuous effort is like compounding interest - it adds up. You need passion, preparation and persistence to succeed. The most important 'P' is however PERSISTENCE!

WISDOM NUGGET #17: Hard practice, easy game.
Easy practice, hard game.

April 1
"Every time you are tempted to act in the same old way, ask if you want to be a prisoner of the past or a pioneer of the future."– Deepak Chopra
A great lesson to learn is that your past does not have to be your future. You can start today to make your future bright. Get going!

April 2
"Patience is the calm acceptance that things happen in a different order than the one you have in mind." – David G. Allen
Sometimes you have to wait. It takes time for the seeds you planted to grow. And sometimes the fruits of your labor don't arrive when expected. Be flexible!

April 3
"God makes oranges. God doesn't make orange juice."– Rev. Jesse Jackson
We have been given so many gifts in this world to make great things. But the work doesn't get done for us. Get busy doing the work to make great things. If you want juice you have to squeeze the orange!

April 4
"Once a word has been allowed to escape, it cannot be recalled."
– Horace
Think about what you say before you say it. Weigh your words carefully so you don't regret them later. If you can't improve the conversation, stay silent. Taste your words before you spit them out!

April 5
"Sometimes letting things go is an act of far greater power than defending or hanging on." – Eckhart Tolle
You should hang on when the storms of life hit you. But sometimes you need to let go of things too. Let go of what no longer serves you, especially toxic people & things!

April 6
"I have sometimes been wildly, despairingly, acutely miserable, but through it all I still know quite certainly that just to be alive is a good thing." – Agatha Christie
You are still breathing. Be grateful just for that. On its worst days life still gives us opportunities & hope!

April 7
"Stay committed to your decisions, but stay flexible in your approach." – Tony Robbins
Planning is important but the plan isn't. Stay committed to your goals but always be open to different ways of achieving them. There's more than one path to the success you have planned for!

April 8
"Spirit has 50 times the strength and staying power of brawn and muscle." – Mark Twain
It's not the strongest who survive, it's the most resilient. Keep spirits up. Circumstances shouldn't control how you think & feel; how you think & feel can control circumstances. Have faith!

April 9
"To bring anything into your life, imagine that it's already there." – Richard Bach
Acting as if you already have something you want helps you attract what you want. Have a clear vision for your life and imagine you are already living it. A vision helps make it a reality!

April 10
"A grateful mind is a great mind which eventually attracts to itself great things." – Plato
Develop an attitude of gratitude on a daily basis. It will lead you to attracting more great things into your life. You'll get more of what you love if you love what you already have!

April 11
"The supreme accomplishment is to blur the line between work and play." – Arnold Toynbee
If your job is as much fun as your play, you have it made. You'll work harder & longer because it's not really work to you. Find your passion then find a way to make your passion your work!

April 12
"What is important is seldom urgent, and what is urgent is seldom important." – Dwight D. Eisenhower
Don't live your life like everything is an emergency. It isn't. Do the things that really matter to you first. Ask yourself – is this really urgent? Do what's important first!

April 13
"I am not often aware that I am happy. But I often remember that I have been happy." – Robert Fulghum
We look back all the time and remember the good old days. All the days of your life are the good old days in retrospect, so enjoy them while they are happening!

April 14
"We all have the time; the question of the quality of life is answered by how we spend it." – Anthony Robbins
Don't ever say you don't have the time. We all have 24 hours a day; it's how we use it. All time you spend should be quality time! Make the best of all of your moments.

April 15
"We are more interested in making others believe we are happy than in trying to be happy ourselves." – Francois de la Rochefoucauld
Stop trying to keep up with the Joneses. They are probably trying to keep up with you. The only person you need to impress in your life is you!

April 16
"It is better to be prepared for an opportunity and not have one than to have an opportunity and not be prepared." – Whitney Young Jr. Have a plan before opportunity arrives. When it does come it is too late to prepare. Start preparing now. Always be ready for any opportunity!

April 17
"Take it easy, but take it." – Woody Guthrie
Be relaxed and confident when going after your goals. Detach from the results. Be mindful of the process. BUT - go and get them if you really want them. Go after what you want like you're chasing down the last bus of the night!

April 18
"I know of no more encouraging fact than the unquestionable ability of man to elevate his life by conscious endeavor." – Henry David Thoreau
'If it's to be, it's up to me' is an old adage. It is true, and it's the best news possible for you. You really can do it yourself!

April 19
"The purpose of life is the expansion of happiness." – Maharishi Mahesh Yogi
It is not selfish to want to be happy. The pursuit of happiness is what life is all about. Decide to be happy! And then help other people be happy too. Spread the joy all over. Life is good!

April 20
"The best way to make your dreams come true is to wake up." – Paul Valery
Stop talking about your dreams and goals and get busy making them a reality. The hardest move in yoga is to get on the mat in the first place. One act beats 10,000 words. Dream with your eyes open!

April 21
"The way I see it, if you want the rainbow, you gotta put up with the rain." – Dolly Parton
Rainbows only appear to us after it rains. Success only comes after hard work. The sun must set before it rises again. Want something? Then go out and pay the price for it!

April 22
"Nothing will ever be attempted if all possible objections must first be overcome." – Samuel Jackson
There is never a perfect time to start something. There are no guarantees. But if you don't start, you'll never finish. A year from now you'll be sorry you didn't start today!

April 23
"It is not because things are difficult that we do not dare; it is because we do not dare that things are difficult." – Seneca
Everything is hard before it becomes easy. The best motivation is taking action and start making some progress. Dare to begin and you are on your way!

April 24
"When you hire people who are smarter than you are, you prove you are smarter than they are." – R.H. Grant
Successful people aren't threatened by the knowledge of others. They're thankful for it & use it to improve their business. None of us is as smart as all of us together!

April 25
"Progress always involves risk. You can't steal second base and keep your foot on first base." – Frederick Wilcox
Lasting success always requires some degree of calculated risk. You don't hit home runs unless you risk going to the plate. Don't settle for good dare to be great!

April 26

"God gives food to every bird, but does not throw it into the nest." – Montenegrin proverb

You can have whatever you want in life. You just have to pay the price for it, and you often have to pay in advance. Nobody will give you success, you have to go out and get it yourself!

April 27

"Be kind, for everyone you meet is fighting a hard battle." – Plato

We all have crosses to bear. We are all facing some sort of difficulties. We all are dealing with some sort of pain at times. Always be kind. We're all in this together.

April 28

"The greater danger is not that your hopes are too high and you fail to reach them; it's that they're too low and you do." – Michelangelo

If you are going to dream, dream big. Better to reach high & fall short then reach low & never hit the heights you are capable of!

April 29

"Your mind is yours to control. A musician must make music, an artist must paint, a poet must write, if he be at peace with himself. What a man can be, he must be." – Abraham Maslow

Writers write; singers sing; dancers dance. Do what you love to do and were meant to do.

April 30

"Work can be more fun than fun." – Sir Noel Coward

If your work is something you truly love, it's not even really work to you. Erase the line between what's work and what's play. Do what you really love to do. You'll get more work done that way and have more fun too!

> WISDOM NUGGET #18: The best way to combat stress is to solve the problems that are causing your stress.

May 1
"The tougher you are on yourself, the easier life will be on you." — Zig Ziglar
Hard practice, easy game. Easy practice, hard game. Expect great things from yourself & work hard to get them. If you are disciplined in your work habits every day, great success will come your way!

May 2
"Don't wish it was easier. Wish you were better." — Jim Rohn
Don't pray for a lesser load to carry, pray for a stronger back. Nothing really worth getting comes easy. Achieving your goals doesn't make you great; it's the person you become from working hard at them!

May 3
"As long as you look for a Buddha somewhere else, you'll never see that your own mind is the Buddha." — Bodhidharma
You may not have everything you want in life yet, but you have everything you need. Don't look outside for answers look inside. Have faith in yourself!

May 4
"It is better to be making the news than taking it, to be an actor rather than a critic." — Winston Churchill
Critics have plenty of time. They aren't doing anything themselves, they are just talking about people who are doing things. It's better to play than just be a fan!

May 5

"The trouble with the rat race is that even if you win, you're still a rat." – Lily Tomlin

Life is not a competition. The only person you should be trying to impress is yourself. Stop comparing yourself to others. There is enough in the world to keep everybody happy!

May 6

"The secret of success is making your vocation your vacation." – Mark Twain

Find a job that's so much fun you don't just live for weekends & vacations. When your work becomes your passion your life is better. 40 hours a week are too many to write off waiting for quitting time!

May 7

"All the beautiful sentiments in the world weigh less than a single lovely action." – James Russell Lowell

The world is changed by your actions not by your opinions. The doers are far more valuable to a society than the talkers. Talk really is cheap. Get moving and stop talking!

May 8

"The smallest deed is better than the greatest intention." – John Burroughs

Walk your talk. As Elvis once sang: "A little less conversation, a little more action!" Do what you said you'd do today. Even a small step towards achieving your goals is going in the right direction!

May 9

"It's supposed to be hard. If it wasn't everybody would do it. It's the hard that makes it great." – Tom Hanks

Accomplishing great things takes great effort. It's not easy to get something worth getting, which is why it's so GREAT to finally get it. Everything easy was hard once!

May 10

"Go confidently in the direction of your dreams. Live the life you've imagined." – Henry David Thoreau

It starts with a dream. The dream becomes a clear vision. And the life you've imagined comes after you've done the work. Be confident. Be proud. Go chase your dreams!

May 11

"There are times you can push yourself a little more. You can even surprise yourself." – Pat Quinn

Just when you think you can't do any more is the time to do a little more. Push yourself and do just one more, then one more after that. Surprise! You went from good to great!

May 12

"I couldn't wait for success, so I went ahead without it." – Jonathan Winters

Don't wait for success to come to you. Go out and get success. Start your work and success will follow you. Chase down what you really want in life like you are running after the last bus of the night!

May 13

"Everything that happens to you is your teacher. The secret is to learn to sit at the feet of your teacher and be taught." – Polly Berends

Experience is a tough teacher because it gives the result first, then the lesson. But with the right attitude you either win or learn!

May 14

"Happy is the man who can endure the highest and lowest fortune. He who has endured such vicissitudes with equanimity has deprived misfortune of its power." – Seneca

Getting through bad times will make the good times even sweeter. Adversity is a great teacher, learn from it!

May 15

"In every adversity is a seed of equivalent benefit; it's up to you to find it." – Pat Riley

Look for the good in every adversity. It is there. Find it. Focus on it. You learn more from troubled times than from good times. Tough times don't last but tough people do!

May 16

"Everything can be taken from a man but one thing; the last of human freedoms – to choose one's attitude in any given set of circumstances, to choose one's own way."– Victor Frankl

The greatest freedom is the ability to choose our attitude. That is always up to us!

May 17

"Success is not the key to happiness. Happiness is the key to success." – Albert Schweitzer

You choose happiness. It's the starting point of a healthy mental lifestyle. Circumstances shouldn't dictate your mood your mood should dictate your circumstances. Choose happy first!

May 18

"When you change the way you look at things, the things you look at change." – Wayne Dyer

We don't always need to see new things we just need to see the same things with different eyes. Look at your life differently. Focus on the good. Reality is your perception of it!

May 19

"You don't learn anything when you are talking." – Larry King

The things you can do to learn are: reading, studying, listening and by getting out there and doing what you want to do. You don't learn anything when you talk - you just repeat what you already know!

May 20
"Because if you don't know, life is made up of moments. Don't lose the now." – Jorge Luis Borges
This moment isn't a prelude to something else. It's your life. There's only NOW so don't lose the moment. Don't live yesterday, today and tomorrow at once. We only have moments to live!

May 21
"Whatever you want to do, do it now." – Michael Landon
There is no better time to do something you really want to do than NOW. That's not reckless, and sometimes extensive planning is required, but the message is - don't wait. A year from now you'll wish you had started today!

May 22
"Losing is a learning experience. It teaches you humility. It teaches you to work harder. It's also a powerful motivator." – Yogi Berra
Losing does not make you a loser. It makes you a player who has had a temporary setback. You win or you learn with the right attitude to it!

May 23
"Don't count the days, make the days count." – Muhammad Ali
It's not the years in your life that define you; it's the life in your years. Make every day count. Even in tough times don't wish the days of your life away. Focus on what you can do, not on what you can't!

May 24
"If you correct your mind, the rest of your life will fall into place." – Lao Tzu
Your life becomes a reflection of your thoughts. When you really realize the power of optimism, your life will change for the better dramatically. Train your mind to serve you better!

May 25

"Some things have to be believed to be seen." – Ralph Hodgson

You don't need belief to see things that are right in front of you. But if you truly believe that you will get something you really want, you are already halfway to getting it. Believe it - then you'll see it!

May 26

"Become a possiblitarian. No matter how dark things seem to be or actually are, raise your sights and see possibilities. Always see them, for they're always there." – Norman Vincent Peale

Even when you hit rock bottom, you can still look upwards. Open up all the possibilities!

May 27

"I always wondered why somebody didn't do something about that. Then I realized I was somebody." – Lily Tomlin

Looking for somebody to do something about that? Then look in the mirror. You be the person that does something about that. We are the change that we seek.

May 28

"We learn from experience that men never learn from experience." – George Bernard Shaw

Your experiences are a great teacher for you - but only if you choose to learn from them. Are you living and learning every day? If so you never lose. Learn from all of your mistakes!

May 29

"If you're going through hell, keep going." – Winston Churchill

As hard as it can be at times, the best thing to do when going through troubled times - is to keep going. Keep moving. Keep swinging. Don't sit down and grieve, stand up and face them. You will come through stronger!

May 30
"You can preach a better sermon with your life than with your lips."
— Oliver Goldsmith
You are not judged by what you say but by what you do. Have a passionate belief about something? Then let your actions do the talking. One action is better than 1,000 words & is louder!

May 31
"Never take one day for granted. It's a privilege to be standing here today. It's a blessing." — Chuck Pagano
It is a privilege to have to face some problems from time to time, because it means you are still alive to face them. Be grateful that you are still in the game!

> WISDOM NUGGET #19: Not being grateful for something is like not even really having it.

June 1
"The longer we dwell on our misfortunes the greater their power to harm us." — Voltaire
It's not easy facing bad times. But dwelling on them does nothing, it only increases our pain. Don't allow yourself to suffer over & over again over the same misfortune. Focus on what is good!

June 2
"Bitterness is like drinking poison and waiting for the other person to die." — Steve Ostten
The only person who is hurt by you being bitter is you. Lingering bitterness serves no purpose at all. Learn to just move on from things you don't like. Don't be bitter, be better!

June 3

"If you have the time to whine and complain about something then you have the time to do something about it."– Anthony J. D'Angelo
If people took all the time they spent on complaining and did something about what they were complaining about – they'd have less to complain about!

June 4

"A man who sees the world the same at 50 as he did at 20 has wasted 30 years of his life." – Muhammad Ali
If you aren't learning you aren't growing. And if you aren't growing, then you aren't really living. Examine your beliefs and update if necessary!

June 5

"It's kind of fun to do the impossible." – Walt Disney
The word impossible is actually also "I'm possible" – people who are doing the impossible shouldn't be interrupted by the people who don't think it's possible. Dream big things and do big things!

June 6

"The indisputable first step in getting the things you want out of life is this: decide what you want." – Ben Stein
The biggest reason people don't have what they want in life is – they don't know what they want. You need to have a dream before you can make it happen. Dream big!

June 7

"Happiness is available...please help yourself." – Thich Nhat Hanh
When you really come to understand how so much of how you feel is up to you, you will immediately start to feel better. That knowledge is life-changing. Happiness is free & you can always choose your attitude!

June 8
"If not you, who?
If not here, where?
If not now, when?"
- Theodore Roosevelt

The answers are:
You...
Wherever you are...
NOW...
Don't postpone your life. If it's to be it's up to me - and the ME in this case is YOU! It is YOUR time right NOW right where you are!

June 9
"As he thinks, so is he; as he continues to think, so he remains." – James Allen
You create your reality by the way you think. When you come to understand how powerful your thoughts really are, you'll focus on thinking positive. Choose to look for the good things in life!

June 10
"The strength of the team is each individual member. The strength of each member is the team." – Phil Jackson.
We do not accomplish great things alone. There is enormous power in working together & relying on your TEAMMATES. Please join our team!

June 11
"Problems cannot be solved by thinking in the framework in which they were created." – Albert Einstein
There is always another way to look at & tackle any problems you face. Take a step back. Explore new ways to solve them. Try a different approach to get different results!

June 12

"All the adversity I've had in my life, all my troubles and obstacles, have strengthened me...You may not realize it when it happens, but a kick in the teeth may be the best thing in the world for you." – Walt Disney

You succeed because of adversity, not despite it. Win or learn!

June 13

"Too often in life, something happens & we blame other people for us not being happy or satisfied or fulfilled. So the point is, we all have choices, & we make the choice to accept people or situations or to not accept situations." – Tom Brady

Only accept the best for yourself!

June 14

"Obstacles don't have to stop you. If you run into a wall, don't turn around and give up. Figure out how to climb it, go through it, or work around it." – Michael Jordan

Obstacles are things you see when you take your eyes off your goals...always a way through or around them!

June 15

"Don't be afraid to give up the good to go for the great." – John D. Rockefeller

A chunk of coal under a little more pressure becomes a diamond. The difference between tri and triumph is just some "umph"! Passion. Preparation. PERSISTENCE! That's how you turn good into great!

June 16

"My motto was always to keep swinging. Whether I was in a slump or feeling badly or having trouble off the field, the only thing to do was keep swinging." – Hank Aaron

Home run champs also strike out a lot. But when you keep swinging, you hit a lot of homers!

June 17

"Big shots are little shots who just kept shooting." –
Christopher Matey
One thing all successful people have in common - PERSISTENCE.
They keep going. You don't have to be smart or rich to have persistence, you just have to keep going. Faith it to make it!

June 18

"Each morning we are born again. What we do today is what
matters most." – Buddha
Every day is a chance to start fresh. Every day is another opportunity to do the right thing. Celebrate each new day as a chance to
be better!

June 19

"It's how you approach it every single day that puts you in a position
to succeed. It's about winning the day, every day." – LeBron James
Give the world your best today. Approach today like it's the most
important one in your life...because it is. Just win the day today!

June 20

"When you do the things you need to do, when you need to do them,
the day will come when you can do the things you want to do, when
you want to do them." – Zig Ziglar
Before you do what you want to do, do what you need to do. Life
gives you what you want when you pay in advance!

June 21

"Life is just a lot better if you feel you're having 10 wins a day rather
than a win every 10 years or so." – Astronaut Chris Hadfield
Celebrate all of your wins along the way to reaching your goals.
Simple pleasures are great too. You can't go into space every day of
the year!

June 22
"Perpetual optimism is a force multiplier...Spare me the grim litany of the 'realist;' give me the unrealistic aspirations of the optimist any day." – Colin Powell
Optimists live longer and they live better. Pessimism drains, optimism empowers. Believe it and you'll see it!

June 23
"There are only two options regarding commitment; you're either in or you're out. There's no such thing in life as in-between." – Pat Riley
Are you truly committed to reaching your goals? Then go after them like you're chasing after the last train of the night! Go all in!

June 24
"Inaction breeds doubt & fear. Action breeds confidence & courage. If you want to conquer fear, do not sit home and think about it. Go out & get busy." – Dale Carnegie
Movement creates motivation, not the other way around. Take your fears on head on. Taking action empowers you!

June 25
"Don't settle for the passenger seat if you really want to drive the car." – Oprah Winfrey
Go for what you really want. Life is too short to play small, or settle for less than what you are capable of. Dream big this week. You are the driver of your life!

June 26
"The journey is the reward." – Steve Jobs
Don't wait to be happy and satisfied with your life or career. You can be deeply grateful and still striving for better at the same time. Gratitude and ambition are not opposites. Enjoy all the moments on the road to a better life!

June 27
"To really enjoy life, you must get out of your head and live in the moment." – Lonnie Ali
Don't live yesterday, today and tomorrow all at once!

June 28
"Obstacles are those frightful things you see when you take your eyes off your goal."- Henry Ford
Focus on your goals, not on your obstacles. Create a vision for how you want your life to look and keep working at it. Enjoy the process of being a work in progress - everybody is!

June 29
"Nothing splendid has ever been achieved accept by those who dared believe that something inside them was superior to circumstance." – Bruce Barton
You are not defined by your job or any of your other circumstances. Don't let rough times define you, make them refine you!

June 30
"The only time you have to succeed is the last time you try." – Philip H. Knight
The stonecutter hammers at a rock 100 times without a crack, until the 101st time when it splits in two. That blow didn't do it, it was what came before. Keep pounding the rock & success will come!

WISDOM NUGGET #20: If your best friend was facing the issue you are facing what would you tell them? Take your own advice!

July 1
"Every strike brings me closer to the next home run." – Babe Ruth
The home run king strikes out a lot. He fails a lot. That's because he's up there at the plate swinging instead of sitting on the bench. When he connects – home run! Want some homers in life? Step up to the plate!

July 2
"Whatever you can do or dream you can, begin it. Boldness has genius, power and magic in in it." – Goethe
Take the first step. Get started on something you really want to do. Action creates momentum, not the other way around. Be bold this week: show the world what you are made of!

July 3
"If you think you can do a thing or think you can't do a thing...you're right." – Henry Ford
The first step to improving yourself is to believe in yourself. We all have untapped potential inside just waiting to be used. If you think you can - you can. Now make It happen!

July 4
"You're braver than you believe, stronger than you seem and smarter than you think." – Christopher Robin
Believe in yourself. There is potential in everyone to do great things. Sometimes we're our own worst enemies. Be your own best friend & faith it to make it!

July 5
"The main thing is to keep the main thing the main thing." – Stephen Covey
It's not the number of things on your "To Do List" that get done, it is how many of your priorities get done. Spend your time & energy on the things that really matter first!

July 6
"It is better to light a single candle than to curse the darkness." – Eleanor Roosevelt
Complaining about your circumstances accomplishes nothing. Taking actions, even small ones, can often accomplish a lot. Don't sit & curse the dark. Turn on a light & expect brighter days!

July 7
"Where so ever you go, go with all your heart." – Confucius
There are no degrees of commitment. You are either committed to doing something or you are not. Whatever you do, bring all you have to it. The world deserves your very best!

July 8
"Your attitude, not your aptitude, will determine your altitude." – Zig Ziglar
Having a natural ability to do something is great. But how high you'll fly in life is more determined by how you look at things. Have an attitude of gratitude - and the sky's the limit!

July 9
"It is good to have an end to journey to, but it is the journey that matters, in the end." – Ursula K. Le Guin
The best thing about setting goals is the person you become as a result of going after them. Reaching the summit is great but don't miss out on the journey to it!

July 10
"I never met a bitter person who was thankful. Or a thankful person who was bitter." – Nick Vujicic
Count your blessings not your troubles. Choose to be better not bitter. Develop an attitude of gratitude & the bitterness will disappear.

July 11
"Action is the antidote to despair." – Joan Baez
When dark moods hit you, it always helps to get up and move. Don't just sit and mope. Get busy. Be active. Stand up tall and face your troubles straight in the eye - they don't look as big that way!

July 12
"It takes no more time to see the good side of life than to see the bad." – Jimmy Buffett
Glass half full or glass half empty? Partly sunny or partly cloudy? Life is all in how you look at. Optimism is just as "realistic" as pessimism is. Choose optimism. You'll live longer!

July 13
"I'm a big fan of dreams. Unfortunately, dreams are our first causality in life - people give them up, quicker than anything, for a 'reality.'– Kevin Costner
Turn your dreams into reality. Follow them & go after your goals with everything you have!

July 14
"Don't judge each day by the harvest you reap, but by the seeds you plant." – Robert Louis Stevenson
Patience isn't just sitting around; it's giving time to let the seeds of your labor grow. Water doesn't boil any faster by you staring at it! Want more fruit? Plant more trees!

July 15
"Everyone wants to live at the top of the mountain, but all the happiness and growth occurs while you are climbing it." – Andy Rooney
Ask any mountain climber: if the only thing that mattered was the view at the top of the mountain, they'd take a helicopter! Enjoy the process!

July 16

"Your time is limited. Don't waste it living somebody else's life." — Steve Jobs

The only person you need to satisfy by the way you live is you. Be grateful & generous with what you have, but when it comes to how you live your life - YOU do YOU!

July 17

"Avoid negative people at all costs. They are the greatest destroyers of self-confidence & self-esteem." — Brian Tracy

Too often we spend too much time arguing with people we don't even know or like on social media. Why? Spend time with those who uplift you, not who degrade you!

July 18

"Most of the successful people I've known are the ones who do more listening than talking." — Bernard Baruch

Listening is wanting to hear. You don't learn anything by talking you just repeat what you already know. One action equals 1,000 words, so do more, talk less & listen!

July 19

"There will always be rocks in the road ahead of us. There will be stumbling blocks or stepping stones, it depends on how you use them." — Friedrich Nietzsche

We all face obstacles on our path. Rock in your way? Move it or use it. Win or learn!

July 20

"Because while you are imagining, you might as well imagine something worthwhile." — L.M. Montgomery

We often tend to imagine the worst. Why? Imagine the best! Fact: optimists live longer & feel better. The power of positive psychology is science. Believe it and you'll see it!

July 21
"Your life is an occasion. Rise to it." – Suzanne Weyn
If you want to do something important with your life, start today.
Every new day is a new opportunity to rise and shine. Treat every
day like it's a special occasion...because it is!

July 22
"If one only wished to be happy, this could be easily accomplished;
but we wish to be happier than other people, & this is always
difficult, for we believe others to be happier than they are."
– Montesquieu
The grass isn't greener on the other side it's greener where you
water it!

July 23
"Never confuse a single defeat with a final defeat." – F.
Scott Fitzgerald
The only people that never lose at anything are those who never do
anything. There is great data in failure. Pick up after a loss and get
back in the game. Fall seven. Rise eight!

July 24
"Do not anticipate trouble, or worry about what may never happen.
Keep in the sunlight." – Benjamin Franklin
Want to test your memory? Try to remember what you were
worrying about a year ago. Most worries never actually happen. The
answer to dark times is to look for a light!

July 25
"In the battle between the river & the rock, the river will always win.
Not through strength but by persistence." – Buddha
You can accomplish great things when you keep going. The river
will eventually wear down the rock. 3 Ps to success: Passion.
Preparation. PERSISTENCE!

July 26
"It will never rain roses: when we want to have more roses, we must plant more roses." – George Eliot
Take some action today to make your life better. Action creates momentum. Plant some seeds for future success & give them time to grow. Then watch those roses bloom!

July 27
"You will face many defeats in your life, but never let yourself be defeated." – Maya Angelou
No defeat is permanent. Every day presents you with another opportunity to win again. Learn from defeat and move on from it. Get right back in the game!

July 28
"Before you speak ask yourself if what you are about to say is true, is kind, is necessary, is helpful. If the answer is no, maybe what you are about to say should be left unsaid." – Buddha
Better to stay quiet today than to have to apologize tomorrow. Be kind with your words!

July 29
"Man stands in his own shadow and wonders why it's dark." – Zen proverb
Don't curse the darkness, light a candle. The way out of a dark situation is to look for the light. As the Beatles said "Tomorrow it may rain so, I'll follow the sun." Good advice!

July 30
"Treat every moment as your last. It is not preparation for something else." – Shunryu Suzuki
The best way to slow down time is to stop trying to live yesterday, today & tomorrow all at once. Live in the moment. Take a deep breath. Now is the perfect time!

July 31
"Life is not a spectator sport." – Jackie Robinson
Live your life to the fullest. If you aren't sleepy by the end of the day, then you didn't use the day to its maximum. Stop criticizing and do what you need to do to make your life better. Get out of the stands and into the game!

> WISDOM NUGGET #21: Being deeply grateful and being very ambitious are not opposites; be grateful and you'll have more to be grateful for.

Aug. 1
"Do not spoil what you have by desiring what you have not; remember that what you now have was once among the things you only hoped for." – Epicurus
You have things now that you used to only wish you had. Count your blessings not your troubles. You are richer than you think!

Aug. 2
"The difference between hope & despair is a different way of telling stories from the same facts." – Alain de Botton
We don't get sad about events, we get sad about the way we interpret events. It's all in how you look at it. Not everything is good, but there's good in everything!

Aug. 3
"If you want others to be happy practice compassion; if you want to be happy practice compassion." – Dalai Lama
You get back what you give. The way you act towards people is how they'll react to you. Give to others what you want others to give to you!

Aug. 4
"Rock bottom became the solid foundation on which I rebuilt my life." – J.K. Rowling
When you think you've tried everything to succeed, remember - you haven't. The only time you HAVE to succeed is the last time you try. Being at "rock bottom" just makes for a better success story!

Aug. 5
"You may not control all the events that happen to you, but you can decide not to be reduced by them." – Mayu Angelou
You learn more from defeat than you do from victory. There is great data to be taken out of every setback. No defeat is ever permanent!

Aug. 6
"What you seek is seeking you." – Rumi
The things we want come to us easier when we are open to the possibility that those things are seeking us, maybe even more than we seek them. What you are looking for, someone else needs you to get. Positive energy is like a magnet!

Aug. 7
"One of the greatest discoveries a man makes, one of his greatest surprises, is to find he can do what he was afraid he couldn't do." – Henry Ford
Face your challenges head on this week. When you stand up to your problems you look bigger & they look smaller. Discover your power!

Aug. 8
"The more you depend on forces outside yourself, the more you are dominated by them." – Harold Sherman
We look outside ourselves for answers when we should be looking inside. What happens to us isn't as important as what we think about what happens to us. Believe in yourself!

Aug. 9
"My belief is stronger than your doubt." – Dwayne Wade
Believe in yourself. If you don't, surround yourself with people who
believe in you until you do; they'll help you get there. And when you
do - stay surrounded by the same people! Faith it to make it!

Aug. 10
"The people who get ahead in this world are the people who get up
and look for circumstances they want, and if they don't find them,
make them." – George Bernard Shaw
Open up all the possibilities to make your life better. Get out in the
world and show people what you can do!

Aug. 11
"The more you sweat in the gym, the less you bleed in the ring." –
Sugar Ray Leonard
The Summer Olympics are won in the winter, and vice versa. The
work you do when nobody is watching pays off when everybody is.
Be prepared. Hard practice, easy game. Easy practice, hard game!

Aug. 12
"You are more important than your problems." – Jose Ferrer
Some challenges you face are daunting and are important to deal
with. But your problems are not more important, or GREATER, than
you are. Don't let any issue make you think you can't rise above it.
Stand tall!

Aug. 13
"What the caterpillar calls the end, the rest of the world calls a
butterfly." – Lao Tzu
Just when you think you've reached the end, you may find out it's a
new beginning. It is darkest before the dawn after all. Your turn to
fly high may be just around the corner!

Aug. 14
"What happens is of little significance compared with the stories we tell ourselves about what happens. Events matter little, only stories of events affect us." – Rabih Alameddine
Bad situations are made worse by ruminating about them. Live in the moment. Everything is temporary!

Aug. 15
"I am bigger, better than I thought. I did not know I had so much goodness." – Walt Whitman
Only one person can give you self-esteem. YOU. Mentors are great & helpful, but your life changes once you become your biggest advocate. Self-love is not selfish. Be your own biggest fan!

Aug. 16
"Never give up on what you really want to do. The person with the big dreams is more powerful than the one with all the facts." – H. Jackson Brown Jr.
Discover what you love to do, then go out and do it. Believe in yourself. Faith it to make it!

Aug. 17
"No life is so hard that you can't make it easier by the way you take it." – Ellen Glasgow
A positive mindset makes difficult situations more bearable. It doesn't solve your problems but it helps you deal with them better. Optimism helps your thinking!

Aug. 18
"Each time we face our fear, we gain strength, courage and confidence in the doing." – Theodore Roosevelt
When you stand up to your fears they shrink. You get bigger and they look smaller. Confidence comes from doing not from thinking. You are stronger than you think you are!

Aug. 19
"Give every day the chance to become the most beautiful day of your life." – Mark Twain
Not every day is great but there is great in every day. Look for the good in everything that comes your way. Optimism is infectious!

Aug. 20
"Begin to be now what you will be hereafter." – William James
Every new week, new month, new year & new day is an opportunity to start over. The best time to begin improving your life is NOW. Here's to new beginnings, go get 'em!

Aug. 21
"There is no practice more degrading, demeaning & soul destroying than that of self-pity." – James Allen
People with self-esteem have no time for self-pity. Stand tall. You're a survivor. You are stronger than you think & bigger than any problem you face!

Aug. 22
"If you use a different explanatory style, you'll be better equipped to cope with troubled times & keep them from propelling you towards depression." – Martin Seligman
Look at your troubles differently. Optimism isn't blind & it can help you see the light. This too shall pass!

Aug. 23
"It is never too late to be who you might have been." – George Eliot
It's never too late to start and it's always too early to quit. If you are alive you are still in the game. There is still time for you. Stand up tall. Look the world in the eye and show it what you've got!

Aug. 24
"Talent you have automatically. Skill is only developed by hours and hours of beating on your craft." – Will Smith

Talent is natural. Skill is developed. It takes talent, hard work & some luck to really succeed. But the talented, hardworking people seem to get all the luck!

Aug. 25
"Lots of things that couldn't be done have been done." – Charles Austin Bates
Many things seem impossible until somebody does them. Then those accomplishments seemed like they were inevitable anyway. Have faith - then the impossible becomes possible!

Aug. 26
"Breathe. Let go. And remind yourself that this very moment is the only one you know you have for sure." – Oprah Winfrey
We have to breathe to live, but we often don't realize we are breathing. Breathe deep. Smile. Live in the moment. It's a good day for a good day!

Aug. 27
"Ultimately you, and only you, can make yourself consistently happy." – Dr. David D. Burns
Happiness is an inside job. When you understand that you have more control over how you feel than you realize, your life can change. Give yourself permission to enjoy your life more!

Aug. 28
"Contentment is natural wealth, luxury is artificial poverty."
– Socrates
Riches do not make you content. Knowing that riches aren't necessary is what makes you content. And the beauty is the more grateful you are, the more you get to be grateful for.

Aug. 29
"Gratitude at its best is an action." – Henry Timms

Say thank you always. But showing gratitude is much more powerful. One action is worth a 1,000 words. SHOW gratitude for everything in your life!

Aug. 30
"The first step towards getting somewhere is to decide you are not going to stay where you are." – J.P. Morgan
If you are lost & not sure what to do, make one decision today. Decide you are not staying put. Refuse to accept that your circumstances are permanent & get moving!

Aug. 31
"The real voyage of discovery consists not in seeking out new landscapes but in having new eyes." – Marcel Proust
Focus on the solution, not on the problem. Look for the good. Change the way you look at things & the things you look at change. Let gratitude & optimism guide you!

> WISDOM NUGGET #22: Live in the moment. We only have moments to live!

Sept. 1
"What do we live for, if not to make life less difficult for each other?" – George Eliot
Selfless is a much better thing to be than selfish. And the beautiful secret is - the more you give, the more you receive. Help someone today. Be a mentor not a tormentor!

Sept. 2
"You can complain about it, or feel sorry for yourself. But how are you going to make the situation better? – Tony Dungy

Realizing you are primarily responsible for your life isn't frightening, it's empowering. Don't waste time on self-pity; use it on self-improvement instead!

Sept. 3
"It is the trouble that never comes that causes the loss of sleep." – Charles Austin Bates
Want to test your memory? Try to remember what you were so worried about a year ago! Most of our worries never come to be. Stay present. Believe in yourself. Go after your goals this week!

Sept. 4
"You yourself, as much as anybody in the universe deserve your love and affection." – Buddha
Airlines say put your own mask on first. Great advice! You can better help others if you're looked after. Be your own best friend. Self-love isn't narcissism you deserve love too!

Sept. 5
"Failure is not the opposite of success; it's part of success." – Arianna Huffington
Did you fail? Welcome to the club! If at first you don't succeed, you've joined the ranks of some of the world's most successful people. Failure is never final it's just part of the process!

Sept. 6
"The best way to create a feeling if you have it not is to act on every occasion where that feeling is desirable as if you had it already, and soon will have." – Aristotle
See it & you'll believe it. Act like you already have what you want. Visualize it. Faith it to make it!

Sept. 7
"Our greatest glory is not in never falling, but in rising every time we fall." – Confucius

Adversity and defeats are a part of life, especially when you are taking chances and living life to the fullest. Do not fear failure, it's a sign of effort. Fall seven. Rise eight!

Sept. 8
"Time is a created thing. To say 'I don't have time' is like saying 'I don't want to.'"– Lao Tzu
Everybody has the same 24 hours, 7 days a week. Time is not an issue. The choices you make about how you use your time is the issue. Choose wisely!

Sept. 9
"Whatever you're ready for is ready for you." – Mark Victor Hansen
Expect good things to happen. Are you ready for great success? Then get to work on making it happen. What you are longing for is longing for you!

Sept. 10
"This time, like all times, is a very good one if we but know what to do with it." – Emerson
The best time to start making positive changes to your life is now. You don't have to wait for the perfect time because the perfect time is NOW!

Sept. 11
"During the darkest night, act as if the morning has already come."
– Talmud
September 11 was a horrible tragedy we will never forget. But the aftermath showed the incredible power of the human spirit, especially from first responders. Never Forget 9/11 & never forget their bravery.

Sept. 12
"What a wonderful life I've had! I only wish I'd realized it sooner."
– Colette

If we rush through the present moment we miss a lot. We miss our lives. Stop and breathe. Soak in all your moments. Be grateful for the wonderful things in your life NOW!

Sept. 13
"You know, you need mentors, but in the end, you just have to believe in yourself." – Diana Ross
Mentors can help you discover the greatness that is already inside of you. You may not have everything you want yet, but you have everything you need. It's inside you! Believe in YOU!

Sept. 14
"I am where I am because I believe in all possibilities." – Whoopi Goldberg
Open up your mind to new possibilities. Old thinking leads to the same old results. It's not what you look at that matters it's what you see. Believe in yourself & faith it to make it!

Sept. 15
"Well done is better than well said." – Ben Franklin
You change your world by your actions, not by your opinions. One positive action is better than 1,000 words. Talk a little less and do a little more. Walk your talk!

Sept. 16
"Keep your face to the sunshine and you cannot see a shadow." – Helen Keller
Look for the bright side. Stay in the light. The sun is out all day whether we can see it or not. Don't curse the darkness light a candle!

Sept. 17
"The difference between average people & achieving people is their perception of, and response to, failure." – John C. Maxwell

If at first you don't succeed - welcome to the club! Great achievers fail all the time. But there is great data in failure. You either win or learn!

Sept. 18
"The only thing we have power over in the universe is our own thoughts." – Rene Descartes
We can't control circumstances, but we can control how we think about them. And there is nothing "new age" about that concept - Descartes said it 400 years ago!

Sept. 19
"The best way to predict the future is to create it." –
Abraham Lincoln
Don't sit around and wait for good things to happen. Go and make them happen! Live in the moment & if those moments are great, your future will be great too!

Sept. 20
"There is no passion to be found playing small, in settling for a life that is less than the one you are capable of living." – Nelson Mandela
We all dream of a better life. So let's dream big. Have great goals that are worthy of you & get to work on them.

Sept. 21
"The greatest discovery of all time is that a person can change his future by merely changing his attitude." – Oprah Winfrey
Is glass half empty or half full? How about you just take a drink & enjoy it? Have an attitude of gratitude!

Sept. 22
"The greatest weapon against stress is our ability to choose one thought over another." – William James

You are not responsible for every thought that comes into your head, but you are responsible for the ones you let sit there. Take charge of your thoughts. They are not all facts!

Sept. 23
"Set peace of mind as your highest goal and organize your life around it." — Brian Tracy
The most important goal for yourself should be to live the life you want to live. If you have peace of mind, everything else falls into place. Calm your mind & your life will be calmer!

Sept. 24
"If people just took it one day at a time, they'd be a lot happier." — Stephen King
Don't live yesterday, today & tomorrow at the same time. Breathe deep. Live in the moment. We only have moments to live!

Sept. 25
"Dreams are made possible if you try." — Terry Fox
He was the greatest athlete of all-time, 143 marathons in as many days. But Terry Fox was also our greatest inspiration. Start where you are. Believe in yourself. Go live your dreams!

Sept. 26
"Faith is the bird that feels the light and sings when the dawn is still dark." — Rabindranath Tagore
The bird that starts singing before the sun rises knows it will soon. So just because you can't see a solution to your issues now doesn't mean they're not there. Have faith!

Sept. 27
"Could we change our attitude, we should not only see life differently, but life itself would come to be different." — Katherine Mansfield

You can't change the world, but you can change your attitude to the world. If you do that, your world will change.

Sept. 28
"What to do with a mistake; recognize it, admit it, learn from it, forget it." – Dean Smith
Mistakes happen. But never beat yourself up over them; they are a part of growing & learning. With the right attitude you always either win or learn!

Sept. 29
"The moment of victory is far too short to live for that and nothing else." – Martina Navratilova
The moment you finally achieve a goal is far too short to live for with nothing else. Embrace the process and the journey. The road to success is where all the joy is!

Sept. 30
"Pain is inevitable. Suffering is optional." – Buddha
We all have pain at times. But we don't have to suffer. Reach out if you need to. You are not alone. There is something in you that the world needs or you wouldn't be here. You are loved!

WISDOM NUGGET #23: Optimistic people
have pessimistic thoughts sometimes;
they just don't let them fester.

Oct. 1
"Into each life some rain must fall." – Ella Fitzgerald
Sometimes days aren't great, but there is still great in every day. And a rainstorm isn't a tornado, don't make it into one. The sun will rise again!

Oct. 2

"You can't go back and make a brand new start my friend, but anyone can start from here to make a brand new end." — Dan Zadra
It's never too late to start anew. The time to start making your life what you want it to be is now. Start today. Take a breath - and go make it happen!

Oct. 3

"If you fixate on your worst fear and it comes true, you have lived it twice." — Michael J. Fox
Most of what we worry about never happens, so why worry? When you ruminate about bad things that have happened you are living them over. So live in the moment!

Oct. 4

"Never wrestle with pigs. You both get dirty and the pig likes it." — George Bernard Shaw
Are you spending more time arguing on social media than on using it to learn something, or chat with friends? Why? Stop spending time with people who degrade, look for those who uplift!

Oct. 5

"You can have anything in the world you want if you'll just help enough other people get what they want." — Zig Ziglar
Instead of always asking "What's in it for me?" ask "What's in it for them?" Help people achieve their goals & they'll help you achieve yours. YOU go first!

Oct. 6

"Always be prepared to start." — Joe Montana
When opportunity comes to you, it's too late to prepare. Open up to all the possibilities in your life. Prepare for when one comes and you'll be ready when it arrives. The back-up QB is always ready!

Oct. 7
"I'm realistic. I expect miracles." – Wayne Dyer
You can think big or think small – it takes the same amount of work.
Get into the habit of thinking great things are coming!

Oct. 8
"The secret to getting ahead is getting started." – Mark Twain.
The toughest step in yoga is getting down on the mat to begin.
Action creates momentum so don't wait for momentum to start -
start & you'll develop momentum!

Oct. 9
"Everything you've ever wanted is on the other side of fear." –
George Adair
Stand up to your fears and face them. They look smaller when you
do. Fear knocked at the door. Faith and love answered. There was
nobody there!

Oct. 10
"There is only one way to avoid criticism: Do nothing, say nothing
and be nothing." – Aristotle
Put yourself out there. Say what you mean and mean what you say.
Critics are a dime a dozen but achievers are worth a lot more!

Oct. 11
"If you're lucky enough to do well, it's your responsibility to send the
elevator back down." – Kevin Spacey
The only reason to look down on someone is to help lift them. No
matter how much you have, share it. Sharing shows gratitude & you
get it back!

Oct. 12
"If the only prayer you ever said in your whole life is 'thank you',
that would suffice." – Meister Eckhart

Being grateful is the highest form of prayer. Giving thanks for all you have leads to you getting more as well. A thank you is never misunderstood – so always say THANKS!

Oct. 13
"You either run the day, or the day runs you." – Jim Rohn
How you start the day can make a huge difference in how good a day it is. And as the Navy Seals say MAKE YOUR BED!

Oct. 14
"There is only one success - to be able to spend your life in your own way." – Christopher Morley
Your life is copyrighted by YOU. We all have different definitions of what success means. Live by your terms, not someone else's. Enjoy YOUR life!

Oct. 15
"This is a wonderful day; I've never seen this one before." – Mayu Angelou
Every day is an opportunity to start fresh. You can't change your destination overnight, but you can change your direction. Every day is a special occasion!

Oct. 16
"Stop letting people who do so little for you control so much of your mind." – Will Smith
Look for those who uplift you, not degrade you. Focus on the good people in your life. A critic is someone who says they know the way but can't drive the car themselves!

Oct. 17
"You must do the thing you think you cannot do." – Eleanor Roosevelt

Take the 'T' off can't. Action creates momentum. Get moving & get started on what you need to do & feel your confidence build. You CAN do it!

Oct. 18

"If you want the hits, be prepared for the misses." –
Carl Yastrzemski

The top hitters in baseball fail to get a hit 7 of every 10 times. But they know failure is never final. Keep swinging! That big home run you are looking for may be on the next pitch!

Oct. 19

"Before you hit the jackpot, you have to put a coin in the machine."
– Flip Wilson

Planning is important, but the plan requires action. Get into the game of life. Get moving. Take some chances. You can't win at the game of life if you don't even play!

Oct. 20

"In the middle of difficulty lies opportunity." – Albert Einstein
Open up the possibilities in your thinking when facing difficulties. Look for opportunity. Focus on what you CAN do!

Oct. 21

"Neither failure nor success has the power to change your inner state of being." – Eckhart Tolle

Do your best and then detach from the results. All circumstances are temporary. Failure is never final. With a deep rooted faith in yourself, you either win or learn!

Oct. 22

"The measure of mental health is the disposition to find good everywhere." – Ralph Waldo Emerson

There is always something good, something positive, in the worst of circumstances. Train your mind to look for that good & focus on it. What you focus on expands!

Oct. 23
"Security is not having things, its handling things." – Susan Jeffers
Money does not provide security. Knowing you can manage with or without money is security. Have faith in yourself, that's the security you need. You are bigger than any problem you face!

Oct. 24
"When you are depressed, you wear a pair of eyeglasses with special lenses that filter out anything positive." – David D. Burns, MD.
Not every day is great but there is some great in every day. Focus on what's right not wrong. Count blessings not troubles. Look for the good!

Oct. 25
"You gain strength, courage and confidence by every experience in which you really stop to look fear in the face." – Eleanor Roosevelt
Everything you want in life is waiting for you on the other side of your fears. Stand up to them - they'll look smaller!

Oct. 26
"You miss 100 percent of the shots you don't take." – Wayne Gretzky
The more shots you take at your goals, the more chances you have to hit them. Don't stand on the sidelines, get in the game and create some opportunities for yourself. Then fire away!

Oct. 27
"As I give, I get." – Mary McLeod Bethune
The practice of reciprocity works. Whatever you want most in life, give to someone else. You get back what you give and in many different ways!

Oct. 28

"What other people think of me is none of my business." –
Oprah Winfrey
The most important opinion of you - is the one you have of yourself.
We can be our own worst critics sometimes. Always be your own
best friend and supporter. Cheer yourself up!

Oct. 29

"The key is to keep company with people who uplift you, whose
presence calls forth your best." – Epictetus
The best way to feel encouraged is to be around people who encourage you. Look for those who uplift you and make you better. Hard to
be negative around positive people!

Oct. 30

"That the human spirit is more powerful than any drug. And that
is what needs to be nourished. Work, play, friendship, family.
These are the things that matter. This is what we've forgotten."
Robin Williams
Be kind, as everyone is fighting a battle. And let YOUR spirit shine!

Oct. 31

"Faith is the one power against which fear cannot stand. Day by day,
as you fill your mind with faith, there will ultimately be no room for
fear." – Norman Vincent Peale
Fear knocked on the door. Faith answered. There was nobody there!
Faith it to make it; believe in yourself!

> WISDOM NUGGET #24: When it comes to running
> your business, remember to act like the casino,
> not like the gambler.

Nov. 1
"Happiness is a condition of mind not a result of circumstances." – John Lubbock
Your moods go up and down because your life goes up and down. Kids have it right. They don't need a reason to practice joyful living. Neither do adults. Train your mind to be happy for no reason!

Nov. 2
"Gratitude is not only the greatest of virtues, but the parent of all others." – Cicero
Start each day with a moment of gratitude for everything you have. You'll end each day happier as a result, & soon have more in your life to be grateful for. Count blessings, not troubles!

Nov. 3
"People are not disturbed by events, but by the views they take of them." – Epictetus
Events don't make you unhappy; it's what you think about events that makes you unhappy. Not every day is great but there is some great in every day. Focus on the great!

Nov. 4
"The path is the goal." – Gandhi
The great mountain climbers take a lot of time climbing up & down the mountain & only take a little time to enjoy the view. For them, it's all about the process. It's the journey, not the destination. Walk the path you are on in joy!

Nov. 5
"If winter comes, can spring be far behind?" – Percy Bysshe Shelley
There's a time & a season for everything. Nothing lasts forever; the darkest winter eventually becomes a bright spring. And life isn't about waiting for the storm to pass - it's about learning to dance in the snow!

Nov. 6
"It is one of life's laws that as soon as one door closes, another opens. But the tragedy is that we look at the closed door and disregard the open one." – Andre Gide
There are lots of open doors to walk through to great things. But focus on the one that's shut & you'll miss them!

Nov. 7
"In life there are really no problems, only situations that require a response." – Jon-Kabat Zinn
Frame your problems differently. Focus on solutions. Open up all the possibilities. What you focus on expands so focus on ANSWERS not problems!

Nov. 8
"What lies behind us and what lies before us are tiny matters compared to what lies within us." – Ralph Waldo Emerson
You are stronger than you think. And look for mentors to help, not for tormentors! Focus on the people who uplift you, ignore the haters!

Nov. 9
"You will have bad times, but they will always wake you up to the stuff you weren't paying attention to." – Robin Williams
In bad times you should focus on the good things in your life. Same thing applies in the good times. In bad times & in good, don't take what's good for granted!

Nov. 10
"Be happy for this moment. This moment is your life." – Omar Khayyam
Don't be rushing through the days of your life, it is short enough. This moment isn't just to be rushed through to the next one. Live in the moment. We only have moments to live!

Nov. 11
"Focus on what you have, not on what you lack." – Lou Holtz
What you focus on expands, whether it's good or bad. Look for the good always. A rainstorm isn't a tornado - don't make it one!

Nov. 12
"You know solving other people's problems is easy. The only person I can't seem to figure out is myself." – Thomas James Higgins
If a friend was facing the same difficulties you are right now, what would you tell them? Think about it - then take your own advice!

Nov. 13
"There is no such thing in anyone's life as an unimportant day." – Alexander Woollcott
Every day is an opportunity to do something good. The time of YOUR life is short, make the most of every day. Imagine the possibilities!

Nov. 14
"Success is getting what you want, happiness is wanting what you get" – W. P. Kinsella
Be grateful for what you have & you'll have more to be grateful for. Count your blessings not your troubles. You are richer than you think!

Nov. 15
"If your ship doesn't come in, swim out to it." – Jonathan Winters
Have a vision for your life and once you do, go make it happen! Faith it to make it!

Nov. 16
"Most of us are just about as happy as we make our minds to be." – Abraham Lincoln
Circumstances don't make us sad. Our thoughts about our circumstances do. Every day isn't great but there is great in every day. You can learn to choose a more positive attitude. How liberating!

Nov. 17
"Just keep going. Everybody gets better if they keep at it." —
Ted Williams
The best hitters in baseball fail 6-7 times out of 10. Keep swinging.
Be persistent. Hitting a home run is worth it!

Nov. 18
"Be who you are and say what you feel, because those who mind
don't matter and those who matter don't mind." — Dr. Seuss
Everyone has a unique DNA. Celebrate it. Be YOU...everybody else is
taken! Focus on your supporters, not on your critics!

Nov. 19
"Winners imagine their dreams first. They want it with all their
heart and expect it to come true. There is no other way to live." —
Joe Montana
Have a detailed vision for what you want in life. See it. Feel it. Then
go WORK to make it happen. Believe it & you'll see it!

Nov. 20
"It's not that I'm so smart, it's just that I stay with problems longer."
— Albert Einstein
Persistence will win in the end. Keep working. Keep exploring.
There is always a way to solve problems. Focus on the solution, not
the problem!"

Nov. 21
"Treat yourself as if you're already what you'd like to be." —
Wayne Dyer
Fake it till you make it! Act as if you've already achieved what you're
going after. Have a clear vision for your life & live it daily. Believe it &
you'll see it!

Nov. 22
"Stand up to your obstacles & do something about them. You will find that they haven't the strength you think they have." — Norman Vincent Peale
Stand up to your problems. See? They don't look as big now. Ask for help if you need some. Team up on them!

Nov. 23
"Life goes by fast. Enjoy it. Calm down. It's all funny." — Joan Rivers
Life isn't as serious as our thoughts sometimes make it out to be. Breathe. Relax. Enjoy the moment. Every new day is "the present" - so treat it like one! Focus on the good things in your life! Smile more!

Nov. 24
"It is only possible to live happily ever after on a daily basis." — Margaret Bonnano
Life is made up of moments. Don't wait for the perfect moment to do something, take this moment and make it perfect. Live every moment & the "ever after" looks after itself!

Nov. 25
"Remember that guy who gave up? Neither does anybody else." — Brian Tracy
The biggest difference between success and failure is PERSISTENCE. Good things are coming for you down the road - as long as you don't stop walking!

Nov. 26
"Feeling gratitude and not expressing it is like unwrapping a present and not gifting it." — William Arthur Ward
Always say thank you. The more you say thanks for, the more you'll have to be thankful for. Have an attitude of gratitude!

Nov. 27
"Today I will do what others won't, so tomorrow I can accomplish what others can't." – Jerry Rice
Great success comes at a great price. If you are willing to do what it takes, the sky is the limit!

Nov. 28
"The things I've done in my life have required a lot of years of work before they took off." – Steve Jobs
Nothing happens overnight. But you can get started building a better life overnight. Get started. Keep going. Be persistent! Then "overnight" success comes!

Nov. 29
"What you think of yourself is much more important than what others think of you." – Seneca
The person you need most in your corner to be successful is looking back at you in the mirror. It's called self-worth for a reason. Be your own best friend and biggest advocate!

Nov. 30
"Sometimes the biggest problem is in your head. You've got to believe." – Jack Nicklaus
If you truly believe in yourself, the world will believe in you. And when you truly believe in yourself, you've convinced the person who matters the most. Believe it & you'll see it!

WISDOM NUGGET #25: There is great data
in failure. You either win or you learn.

Dec. 1

"Be miserable. Or motivate yourself. Whatever has to be done, it's always your choice." – Wayne Dyer

Examine your feelings and your beliefs about your life. Choose to focus on the good, not the bad. Pain is inevitable in life but suffering is always optional. Choose optimism!

Dec. 2

"Write on your heart that every day is the best day of the year." – Ralph Waldo Emerson

Not every day is great but there is great in every day. You can't always choose your circumstances but you can always choose how you look at them. Have an attitude of gratitude!

Dec. 3

"The big lesson in life baby is never be scared of anyone or anything." – Frank Sinatra

Everything you want in life is waiting for you on the other side of fear. Stand up to your fears, they'll look smaller. Fear knocked on the door. Faith answered. There was nobody there!

Dec. 4

"If you don't like something, change it. If you can't change it, change your attitude." – Maya Angelou

You can change your circumstances with some dedicated effort. If that's not possible, change the way you think about your circumstances. Focus on the good!

Dec. 5

"What we obtain too cheap, we esteem too lightly; it is dearness only that gives everything its value." – Thomas Paine

Embrace your struggles. Once you get through them you'll appreciate the lesson & what you've accomplished even more!

Dec. 6
"It's not what you look at that matters, it's what you see." — Henry David Thoreau.
Life is how you look at it. Focus on what's right about it & you'll see more to like about it!

Dec. 7
"Remember that there is nothing stable in human affairs; therefore avoid undue elation in prosperity, or undue depression in adversity."
— Socrates
It's not circumstances that make us sad; it's how we react to them. It's all temporary. Focus on what is good!

Dec. 8
"It is not how much we have, but how much we enjoy, that makes happiness." — Charles Spurgeon
If you aren't grateful for the blessings you have, it's like you don't actually have them. Count your blessings not your troubles. Really enjoy what you do have!

Dec. 9
"Love yourself first & everything else falls into line. You really have to love yourself first to get anything done in this world." — Lucille Ball
Self-love is not egotism; it's appreciating yourself as much as you do others. Be your own best friend...you are worthy!

Dec. 10
"Alone we can do so little, together we can do so much." — Helen Keller.
You are not alone in life. Your friends, family & teammates are here to help. None of us is as smart as all of us.

Dec. 11

"1. Don't sweat the small stuff. 2. It's all small stuff." —
Richard Carlson

Don't live your life like everything is an emergency. It's not. Put things into perspective. Have faith, not fear. Not every day is good, but there is some good in every day.

Dec. 12

"There is no health without mental health." — World
Health Organization

The best way to care for your mental health is to care for the mental health of others. Be kinder than necessary. You get back what you give out!

Dec. 13

"There is no way to happiness - happiness is the way." — Thich
Nhat Hanh

You don't find happiness. You tap into it. You don't have to wait for something good to be happy today. Choose to be happy. Focus on the good in every situation. It's there!

Dec. 14

"How little we see! What we do see depends mainly on what we look for." — Sir John Lubbock

When you change the way you look at things, the things you look at change. Sometimes all you need is a new way of looking at the same situation. Look for the good!

Dec. 15

"No one can make you feel inferior without your consent." —
Eleanor Roosevelt

Look for people who encourage you, not those who discourage you. The only reason to look down on someone is to help them up. Focus on the lovers, not on the haters!

Dec. 16
"Gratitude is the place where all dreams come true. You have to get there before they do." – Jim Carrey
Learn to appreciate all that you already have in life. Count the things you have that money can't buy - Family. Friends. Pets. Health. See? You are richer than you think!

Dec. 17
"Once you choose hope, anything is possible." – Christopher Reeve
Once you learn you can choose your attitude towards any circumstances, anything really is possible. Choose faith, not fear; choose hope, not despair.

Dec. 18
"It's not the load that breaks you down, it's the way you carry it." – Lena Horne
Don't wish your life was easier wish you were better. Don't pray for a lesser load to carry, pray for a stronger back. You are more resilient than you think!

Dec. 19
"You can't stop the waves, but you can learn to surf." – Jon Kabat-Zinn
When conquering your problems isn't possible, sometimes all you need to do is just ride them out. Surfers don't conquer waves; they just go with the flow baby!

Dec. 20
"I've lived through some terrible things in my life, some of which actually happened." – Mark Twain
We often imagine bad things that never happen. And even when they do, they are only made worse by how we react to them. Look for the good in every situation - you'll find it!

Dec. 21
"Don't look back. You're not going that way." — Satchel Paige
You can't change the past but you can change the future. The actions you take daily will pay off in the long run. Live well in the moment and your future takes care of itself.

Dec. 22
"Choose to be optimistic. It feels better." — Dalai Lama
You can't always choose your circumstances but you can always choose your attitude towards them. Optimism is not ignoring difficulties it is seeing the good in every difficulty.

Dec. 23
"I will not let anyone walk through my mind with their dirty feet." — Mahatma Gandhi
Surround yourself with people who uplift you, not those who degrade you. Be with a mentor, not a tormentor!

Dec. 24
"Peace on earth will come to stay, when we live Christmas every day." — Helen Steiner Rice
Imagine people acting with the kindness & love they show at Christmas daily. Peace on earth begins with peace in every individual. Do your part. Live Christmas every day!

Dec. 25
"My idea of Christmas, whether old-fashioned or modern, is very simple: loving others. Come to think of it, why do we have to wait for Christmas to do that?" — Bob Hope
Keep the spirit of Christmas in your heart today and every day. Just love one another!

Dec. 26
"If you want to test your memory, try to recall what you were worrying about one year ago today."— E. Joseph Cossman

Many worries never come to be. Think back. What were you worried about last year? Worry takes away from the moment, so live in the moment!

Dec. 27
"You cannot change your destination overnight, but you can change your direction overnight." – Jim Rohn
Don't like the path you are on? Take the first step and turn around. You can change your direction immediately. Focus on where you want to go!

Dec. 28
"Things do not necessarily happen for the best, but some people are able to make the best out of things that happen." – Tal Ben-Shahar
Every day can't be great, but there is great in every day. Count your blessings not your troubles. See? You're richer than you think!

Dec. 29
"Stand up and realize who you are, that you tower over your circum-stances." – Maya Angelou
Any adversity always looks smaller when you stand up to it. You can then really see that you are bigger than any challenge you face. Stand tall!

Dec. 30
"I don't sing because I'm happy, I'm happy because I sing." – William James
Your circumstances don't make you unhappy, what you think about your circumstances makes you unhappy. Momentum follows move-ment. Take action & you'll see!

Dec. 31
"Tomorrow is the first blank page of a 365 page book. Write a good one." – Brad Paisley

Fresh new year & fresh new chance. Open up all the possibilities in your life. Write your story & leave a great legacy. Love your life!

WISDOM NUGGET #26: Planning is important.
The plan isn't.

We post a new quote and inspirational message every day on our Twitter and Facebook accounts; please follow us for some daily inspiration!
@TeammatesTrio on Twitter
@TeammatesTrio on Facebook
EMAIL: teammates@rogers.com

TAKEAWAYS

By now you have read all the blogs and have answered the questions after them with your Personal Development Coach. If you are doing this with a TEAMMATES coach, you've also listened to our audio broadcast from our podcast series. You've read 366 tweets, and you've discussed those with your mentor as well.

Whether you are working with TEAMMATES or not, we hope you have discovered that the key to making these exercises really work for you is working through them with a mentor. We feel that the key component to our work is the individualized personal development coaching in our program. Books and audio programs are great as a stand-alone, but they can't help people deal with the SPECIFIC issues that they are facing. One size does not fit all when it comes to coaching and mentoring; every PDC is different and every client's needs are different.

Those of you who have been through this course with us guiding you have had the benefits of the individual mentoring throughout, and we're confident that you now have the tools and mindset to help you start living better lives and improving in the areas that you want to improve in. You also now have your own Personal Development Coach to help you moving forward, which is the missing ingredient in most self-help programs. For those of you who are just reading the book and/or listening to the audio program on your own, we certainly hope you have found them valuable tools to help you improve your life. The next step for you is to find a mentor that can help you work through this program more fully. You can always contact us later on if you are interested in our TEAMMATES individual personal development coaching, but you can certainly find your own mentor too.

As part of this course for those of you who took it, your TEAMMATES mentorship will be ongoing, and we look forward to continuing to be your teammate for a long time to come. Thank you for having faith in us to allow us to help you achieve your goals and live an improved life.

We want to conclude this course for all of you by providing a general synopsis of what we feel are key elements to take away from our blogs, tweets, audio program and our general philosophy. This will serve as a permanent reference after the course is done, and also be something you can refer to anytime as a refresher.

You have already seen and heard the wide range of topics we have covered, and as we put together this final section for you, we kept in mind that everyone needs an easy reference tool that summarizes the most crucial points of our personal development and growth course.

Our 10 Top TEAMMATES Principles encompass what we've covered here into what we feel are the most important takeaways from the TEAMMATES course that all of you can benefit from. It is also an excellent review for those of you who just purchased the book as a stand-alone so you can continue to benefit from what you have studied.

Read over the following section and refer to it whenever you find yourself drifting a bit from where you want to go in life. These points will serve as reminders on the key points we have touched on and discussed with you, and will summarize the major points we have covered. All good information is worth repeating and summarizing.

We find our clients don't need to be taught as much as they need to be reminded – so use this Top 10 List to help keep you on track as you continue to grow and make your life better in the years ahead.

TOP 10 TEAMMATES PRINCIPLES

PRINCIPLE NO. 1: Be Grateful For What You Have

It all starts with gratitude. Everything does.

That is our firm belief and the foundation of our approach to Personal Development Coaching. The most important thing we hope to help our clients develop as a result of this process is an attitude of gratitude.

If you are not happy with what you have, you won't be happy with what you get. And if you are not truly grateful for the many blessings in your life, it's like you don't even really have them.

Have you ever lost your wallet…or your phone …or some important documents maybe? Go back and think about the absolute panic you went through trying to find the lost article. You looked everywhere for it and thought you'd never find it. But then you did. What a relief - whew!

Now really experience again your sense of absolute relief when your wallet was back in your hands, or your phone, or those documents. You were SO grateful then to have them back in your life, weren't you?

But on a day-to-day basis, do you ever spend even a moment being grateful for having those things in the first place? Do you take them for granted maybe? We are all guilty of that from time to time.

Gratitude must be practiced. It is not enough to only show gratitude when you find your lost wallet. You need to be grateful for having that wallet in the first place.

"But there's never enough money in my wallet!" one client once told us with a laugh. Isn't that the truth for so many of us!

But also in your wallet is your health card, your driver's license, other IDs and your credit cards. Maybe you also carry a photo of a loved one or your pet (and if you don't - why don't you by the way?!). You might bemoan the fact your wallet doesn't have as much money as you'd like in it, but just wait and see how much you'll miss it when you misplace it! Not to mention the hassle you'll have if you have to replace all those important cards. You are carrying great value in your pocket or purse every day and don't even realize it.

Wallets, phones and documents are just things however. The attitude of gratitude is even more important when it comes to your family, friends and health.

Do you know when most people appreciate their health the most? When they get sick and lose their health. Have you ever a broken a limb? If you have I'm sure you can remember the exact moment it happened. But do you remember the day it healed and you were healthy again?

Same goes for when our family or friends have difficulties in their lives, or when we lose them for good. Can you see the common thread here?

"Of course I am grateful!" another client said. "I love my wife and kids."

Then tell them that you love them. And don't wait for a moment of tragedy, or an illness, to really be grateful for the wonderful people already in your life.

So how do we develop this attitude of gratitude that is so important to our foundation of personal development? Glad you asked!

For each one of these Top 10 TEAMMATES Principles we have an exercise for you to do to help make these principles a part of your everyday life. Regular exercise makes your body stronger, and exercising these principles daily makes your mind stronger too.

Exercise No. 1: Make a list of all the good things that are already in your life. Check it daily, in the morning and at night, and say thank you out loud for all you have.

This exercise can do a great deal to lift your mood, especially when you get in the habit of starting and ending your day with a word of thanks. Count up all the things and people you already have in your life. And see how many of those things you counted are things that you wouldn't take any amount of money for.

The old adage says that when the house is on fire, we grab the kids, pets and photos first. The rest of the stuff can be replaced, even that really cool new iPad we just bought or the 60-inch TV.

Our clients generally buy into this principle quickly, but at times we see resistance from the Type A personalities we deal with who feel that being too grateful will make them too complacent.

"I will lose my edge," one client said. "I get it, be more grateful, but won't I then find it harder to have the drive I need to get the things that I want? Success takes motivation, doesn't it?"

While everybody is different, our experience is that truly grateful people don't lose their competitive edge; in fact it's usually the opposite. Practicing gratitude makes them happier, and when they are happier, they generally live longer, work harder and enjoy all stages of their life more.

Gratitude and ambition are not opposites. We constantly work with our clients to make their lives better, for them to work harder and smarter, to set achievable goals that will improve the quality of every aspect of their lives. Loving what you already have doesn't hinder that process, it actually enhances it. And besides, what is the point of constantly striving and never being content with what you already have? Much of what you have now you only dreamt about having years ago after all.

You can be totally grateful - and constantly striving for more - at the same time. Try it. It works.

Count your blessings daily, not your troubles. List all the things in your life that money can't buy. Especially: family, friends, health, pets and those precious mementoes priceless to you alone.

See? You are richer than you think. Principle No. 1 is GRATITUDE. Practice it daily.

PRINCIPLE NO. 2: Live In The Moment

Just live in the moment baby!

We all know that one, right? But like so many things we know we should do, we often don't do it. One of the most common refrains from our clients over the years is that they can't seem to practice mindfulness.

We live yesterday, today and tomorrow all at the same time. We get bogged down in past painful memories and ruminate on them, or we long for a happier future, or we worry that our future is going to be filled with more anguish.

Learning from the past – both the negative and positive things that have happened to us – can be of value. And looking forward to, and planning for, a better future is a healthy way to live too...right?

That's right - but only to a certain extent. Learning from the past and planning for the future is all well and good, but every moment spent LIVING in the past and/or future is robbing you of present moment experiences.

Once of Roger's first clients was an actor. Like a lot of people in that profession, he had lots of trouble making a living from acting, but he loved it none the less. While he worked as a server at a bar to pay his bills, he continued to pursue his true passion which was acting – performing in theatre productions.

His chief problem was missing the moment, unless he was actually on stage. He turned down a role early in his career for personal reasons which he now feels cost him dearly, and he longed for the day when he could stop working as a server so he could pursue acting full time.

His ruminating about past decisions and his obsession with dreaming about the future was robbing him of a lot of joy in his life. He tried to put the past mistakes behind him and tried to stop day dreaming about the future, but he was struggling to do so.

We're happy to report that he was eventually successful in becoming much more present. And ironically enough, his breakthrough happened when he really thought about what he loved most about being on stage and acting in the theatre in the first place.

"When I am on stage, I am fully alive," he said. "I am totally focused on my role, the play, and the moment. Nothing else matters except what I am doing at that second."

Most other actors feel the same way. But how could he manage to be fully present on stage and not at other times? Well it's easier to be fully present when you are doing what you love, but our client came to realize that being on stage in a play doesn't give you any other choice but to be present.

Think about it. You are on stage. The bright lights prohibit you from seeing the audience so you can't look ahead. Behind you is a wall, which is either decorated as a prop or just a black screen, so you can't look behind you. All there is to see and experience is what you are doing at the moment – which is acting in your play. There is nothing to see in front of you or behind you!

"I don't really have a choice but to be 'in the moment' when I'm on stage," our actor client said. "That's how I try to live all the time now."

We only have moments to live. Every second spent in the past or the future robs us of our present moments. So – what do we do to capture that "on stage" feeling on an everyday basis?

Exercise No. 2: Make time daily to just stop and breathe deeply. Meditate. Focus on your breath and just fully experience the moment for a few minutes.

Some of our clients have trouble with this one. They especially shudder when the word meditation is used.

"I can't meditate, I'm no good at it," one client said. "Every time I try to meditate my mind wanders all over the place with all kinds of stupid thoughts! It isn't working for me."

That client is wrong. It is working for him. Every time you stop to breathe and think (call it that instead of meditating if you prefer), you are experiencing mindfulness. And when you catch thoughts going through your head, it's a sign that you are becoming aware of them, which is the first and most important step in the process.

That is all mindfulness really is. It is being aware of the present moment and being aware of your thoughts. What our client didn't realize is those often useless, repetitive thoughts were going through his head all the time anyway – but now he was finally aware of them and could learn to dismiss them. That is what Mindfulness is…being aware of every moment.

You do not meditate to be good at meditation. You meditate to help you live more mindfully. It is not a competition. You are not in the Meditation Olympics. Every time that you have to stop meditating because thoughts are racing through your mind, you are being mindful. Most people who keep at it finally manage to quiet those thoughts, but just realizing that you are not being present is – irony of ironies – being present!

Another one of our clients is a yoga instructor. He has "mastered" the craft of yoga and when he is on the mat, he is in bliss, as are many of his clients. But he came to us after he experienced road rage when driving home from his class one night, if you can believe that. He was in bliss when he was on the mat, but the moment he left his safe environment angry thoughts again started to dominate him.

You do not need to be a yoga or meditation guru to live more mindfully. All you need to do is take the time daily to notice the moment, and live in it more fully. Whether you are "good at it" or not misses the point. If you are becoming more aware, then Exercise No. 2 is starting to work for you.

Another client of ours had to undergo chemotherapy as part of his cancer treatments. He told us that as awful as he felt during that process, the experience certainly taught him how to live in the moment.

"When your body is being scanned, the only thing on your mind is getting through the treatment at that moment," he said. "I wasn't ruminating about the past or wondering how I was going to pay my VISA bill when I was in that tube, believe me!"

The experience, as difficult as it was, did help him greatly. He became more grateful (see Principle No. 1) and he became more AWARE of every moment. He now honestly says that getting cancer and recovering was the best thing that ever happened to him.

Don't wait for a serious illness to focus on the moment you are in. You don't have to sit on a yoga mat, or burn candles, or stare at a Buddha altar to live in the moment either.

Stop reading now. Put the book down and just breathe. Fully experience everything around you and just be. If your mind starts wandering and you notice it wandering – it's working. You are becoming mindful.

Just live in the moment baby!

PRINCIPLE NO. 3: Choose To Be Optimistic

Glass half full or glass half empty?

It's one of the oldest adages around. How do you look at life? Is the glass of water you are holding in your hand half full or half empty? What's your choice?

And before you answer, remember this – it is your CHOICE on how to answer that question.

We deal with a lot of clients, so we hear a lot of different things. But there are certain viewpoints that come up time and time again, and the response to the water glass question has many times garnered this kind of response:

"I want to be an optimist, but I can't help the way I think."

This is where the rubber hits the road friends, especially when it comes to our TEAMMATES Personal Development Coaching program. While we work with a variety of clients and while we understand that not everyone is as far along on their spiritual journey as others are, principle No. 3 must be adhered to if this course is really going to benefit you.

You must give up the belief that you can't help the way you think. You must.

If you truly believe that you can't help the way you think, you have a big problem. And frankly dealing with that problem is better suited for a pay grade higher than ours. We would recommend some psychological counseling for that instead of a Personal Development Coach.

We want to help as many people as we can and we want to work with you, but this is a core belief of ours – if you truly believe you cannot help the way you think – then you will not reach your full potential in your life.

That's a little heavy sounding perhaps, but here's the brighter news for you - you are wrong in thinking you can't help how you think. You CAN help the way you think.

We offer some recommended reading at the end of this workbook for you, and one of our favorites is Martin Seligman. In particular, we believe his book Learned Optimism is one of the best books we've ever read.

Here's the thing about that particular book. It's not pop psychology. It's science. It says that you can rewire your brain to think differently and make your attitude be your choice, whether you want to believe that or not. Dr. Seligman's terrific book explains that in great detail, and we highly recommend it.

"Is it that easy?" a client once asked, when we told her that and handed her a copy of Learned Optimism. Good question.

First of all, who said it's supposed to be easy? Anything worth having in life takes some work and has a certain degree of difficulty to it. Anything really worth having is worth expending some effort for.

So if you think that choosing an optimistic attitude will be "easy" for you, especially if you have been a perpetually negative thinker all of your life, well you are likely to be disappointed. Other people who are already optimists by nature will have little difficulty accepting this principle, as many of them are already living it. But how easy it will be for you to embrace this truth likely depends on how optimistic you are right now.

Choosing optimism is simple. But there is a big difference between simple and easy. And everything that is easy now for you was hard once - right? Watch a baby learn to walk. Watch your grandparents try and figure out a computer. Learning anything is a process and some things are harder than others to learn, and everything is harder the first time we attempt it.

However it starts with wanting to believe your glass is half full. If you make that decision, then it shouldn't be that hard at all to become an optimist.

Now the negative thinkers are reading this and asking – sign me up, but how the hell do I do that?

Another excellent question!

Exercise No. 3: In every situation you face for the next week, stop and ask "Where is the good in this?"

Not every day is good, but there is good in every day. Optimism is not thinking everything is good; it's looking for the good in everything. It is not denying reality; it is looking at your reality in a different way.

You cannot control every thought that comes into your head. But you can control what to do with thoughts when they come. Remember the meditator and the yoga instructor that were struggling with a busy mind in the previous Principle? They calmed their minds by starting to be aware of what they were thinking. First step – they became aware of their thoughts. And after they did that, they then made the CHOICE as to what to do about those thoughts.

Several clients have challenged us on this point. One of Roger's in particular felt that optimism could be dangerous. If someone is overly optimistic, he said, couldn't that lead to ignoring real life problems?

"Isn't it unrealistic to be optimistic?" he said.

We will again turn to Mr. Seligman to answer that question. He perfectly explains how the whole concept of optimism works in his book.

"What we want is not blind optimism but flexible optimism – optimism with its eyes open. We must be able to use pessimism's keen sense of reality when we need it, but without having to dwell in its dark shadows."
– Martin Seligman

Learned optimism is not blind optimism. An optimist does not ignore reality; an optimist just looks at it with completely open eyes. An optimist looks for the good in every situation, focuses on that, and is better equipped to deal with what the reality is as a result.

You cannot control all of your circumstances. But you can control how you react to your circumstances and how you approach them. Being optimistic is a choice you make, and you CAN help how you think.

So back to that glass of water…is it half full or half empty? Well either way, take a sip from it now and for the next week - do Exercise No. 3. As Roger likes to say: LOOK FOR GOOD!

PRINCIPLE NO. 4: Develop a Growth Mindset

Mindset - what a lovely word.

And in recent years it's become a bit of a buzzword to describe those of us who are achieving great things and who are considered mentally strong. Many successful people credit their success to their mindset.

But a mindset can be either helpful to you or hurtful to you. A mindset is the way of thinking we have. It is how we deal with any situation we are facing. Our mindset can either allow us to focus on the opportunities in any situation, or make us focus on the challenges in any situation.

There are lots of books that dig into this topic deeply. But for the purposes of this TEAMMATES Principle, let's just talk about whether you have a fixed mindset or a growth mindset.

It really comes down to belief again: do you believe personal qualities like intelligence and talents are fixed, or are they changeable?

People who have a fixed mindset think we are either born with certain qualities or we're not, and thus we cannot change them. People who have a growth mindset believe that these qualities can be developed and are fully changeable with hard work and a commitment to improving.

Since you have made it this far in this course, you clearly know where TEAMMATES stands on this issue. We believe a growth mindset can be developed and improved upon, and we also believe it is crucial to have a strong growth mindset and not a fixed mindset.

Jim, Chris and Roger love stories. As you heard in the audio portion of this course if you took it, or if you have ever listened to our podcast series, you know that already. One of our favorite stories revolves around a woman who works as an Executive Host for one of the big hotel chains in Las Vegas.

She definitely has a growth mindset. She is always "on" as the saying goes. She is constantly focused on growth and refuses to let any negative circumstances get in the way of her continuing to build her portfolio of high rolling clients that come to her hotel.

There is nothing "natural" about this way of thinking she has; her mindset was developed by her practicing it over the years. She was not a "natural" at sales or marketing or "born to sell" - she just developed and honed her skills and her growth mindset due to an incredible worth ethic. She always focuses on the opportunities in any given situation, instead of the drawbacks.

OK now to the story...

One night Susan was coming out of the parking garage of a competitor's hotel, located across the Strip from the hotel she worked at. There was a long lineup of cars trying to exit, and her car was sixth in line to get to the gates to exit the garage.

Her companion was fuming. He cursed the fact they had to wait in line and was miserable about the experience. He turned to Susan to continue his moaning only to see her suddenly bolt from the car and head directly to the car in front of them.

"Where the hell is she going?!" said Susan's companion to their driver, who was equally surprised watching from the front seat.

Susan knocked on the window of the car in front of them. The driver rolled it down and they had a brief conversation. Susan handed the driver her business card and repeated the process with the other five cars ahead of them in the line before returning to her own vehicle.

"What the hell were you doing?" said her companion.

Susan explained what she did while they waited to make their way through to the exit. She went to the six cars in front of them, knocked on the window and spoke with each driver. She told them that her hotel's garage didn't have long lineups like this and next time, they should stay there! She simply smiled and handed out her business card to all six drivers and used the opportunity to get in a quick plug for her hotel.

Susan has a growth mindset. Instead of just sitting there cursing the delay, she saw the opportunity it presented. Her growth mindset was turned on, looking for any way to improve her business. She saw a way to capture the undivided attention of a potential customer and turn the situation around to her benefit. Her companion was understandably impressed.

He was even more impressed the next day when he came to her office for lunch and saw another example of it. There was a delay in getting a table at the restaurant downstairs, so Susan's companion slumped on the couch to wait for a text to let them know when the table would be ready.

Susan's growth mindset sprang into action again. She pulled out her client list (which contained all kinds of information she'd collected on her customers) and made a phone call while they were waiting for their table.

"Hey Randy how are you?" she started. "We haven't seen you down here in a while. Listen, I have tickets to the Manny Pacquiao fight Saturday, was wondering if you'd like them? Of course they are comps!"

Her companion listened in. In his mind, there was nothing else for him to do but wait slumped on the couch until the message came that their table was ready. Susan, however, saw the delay as an opportunity to make what turned out to be a very profitable phone call.

By the time the text came to notify them the table was ready, Susan had arranged for this high roller to come to her hotel Saturday night in his private jet and bring along nine of his buddies. She knew that he loved boxing from her notes on him, so that was the trigger she used that made him decide to come. Instead of sitting at her desk just waiting for a text, she decided to make a phone call that resulted in a huge sale for her casino.

Her companion was over the top impressed now.

"Boy you have a great mindset Susan. No wonder you are the top seller here," he told her.

"Thanks!" Susan said.

"By the way…how did you ever get tickets to the Pacquiao fight? It's not even being held at this hotel?"

"Oh I don't have tickets to the Pacquiao fight. But honey – this guy will drop a fortune here. So I'll go buy some now!"

That's a great story about someone with a great mindset. Like I said, Susan says she wasn't born with such a powerful sales drive. She developed that mindset.

Want to be like Susan? Want to be a top achiever with a growth mindset that is wired for success? Then try this exercise:

Exercise No. 4: Focus on solutions today, not on your problems. Have a growth mindset when examining your problems.

Whatever the major issue you are facing this week is, stop focusing on the problem and focus on the way to solve it. Look for opportunities in every situation you find yourself in.

Susan's issue was the need to get more customers into her hotel's casino. She had developed a growth mindset by constantly looking at solutions to that – in EVERY situation she found herself in. You can start developing the same kind of growth mindset too with daily practice this week.

Are you stuck in a long commute to work? Take transit instead of driving and send your emails and do other paperwork while somebody else drives you in. You don't have time to listen to your favorite podcasts because you have to clean the house? Listen while you clean. You are not getting enough exercise because you don't have time to go to the gym? Take the stairs to your office instead of using the elevator every single time. Deliberately park your car further away too, so you get a good walk in, or get off the bus or subway one stop sooner.

These are just small examples, but the point is – focus on what you can do and not on what you can't do. Focus on the solution, not on the problem. Don't sit and stew in traffic, use the time to listen to motivational tapes. Get in the habit of looking at every situation in a growth mindset – always ask yourself: 'Where is the benefit in what is happening right now?'

Using your commute time to get a jump on your day on the train or bus instead of driving into work isn't multi-tasking; it's using your growth mindset. So is listening to a podcast while you wash the dishes. What you are actually doing in this exercise isn't as important as the mental muscles you are flexing while doing it. You are training yourself to be in a growth mindset all of the time.

Some people are more naturally inclined to be as useful and as clever as Susan is all the time. But there was nothing really special about Susan… she developed that mindset by staying true to it at all times. It became her default way of thinking.

Have you been worrying about a problem for a long time? Have you been staring at it endlessly, focused on it? Don't focus on the problem; don't focus on the obstacles you are facing (like being stuck in a lineup in your car in a garage). Focus on solutions. Susan always does and that's why she's the best at what she does.

Develop a mindset where you see solutions, not problems. Your growth mindset will only get stronger as you constantly look for different ways to find solutions to the problems you face and you'll make it a habit to think that way. When you change the way you look at things, the things you look at change.

Mindsets aren't inborn. They are developed.

PRINCIPLE NO. 5: Have a Clear Vision

You have to believe it to see it.

That is an old adage turned around, but sometimes you have to believe in something before you can see it. You have to fake it to make it!

A good majority of our clients come to us with a common concern – they don't have what they want in their life yet, so they want to work with a Personal Development Coach to help them get it.

That's certainly a very smart thing to do, whether it is with us or any other good coach or mentor. A problem shared is a problem halved after all.

After doing this for seven years, we have discovered that of all the reasons people reach out to us, the top reason is that they don't have what they want and they want help in getting it. And when a new client comes to us and says that very same thing, we tell them not to worry; many of us don't have what we want in life – not YET anyway! We then ask them this question:

"What do you think the biggest reason people don't have what they want in life is?"

Give that question some thought right now. Of all the clients we've had that have come to us looking to get what they want in life because they don't have it yet, only a very few got the answer to that question right on the first try.

Again – stop and think what the biggest reason people don't have what they want in life is. We've heard all kinds of answers to that question over the years and many of them are excellent.

"They don't work hard enough."

Good answer and yes, a lack of work ethic stops a lot of people from getting what they want.

"They have the wrong attitude."

That's another good answer. As you have already seen from our previous Principles, we are firm believers in the power of having an attitude of gratitude and being optimistic. A poor attitude is indeed a common reason for people not having what they want in life, but it's not number one.

"They lack the money or education they need to succeed."

There is no question that some of the things that people want in life require a lot of money, or a lot of specialized education. Missing "tools" of some kind is another major reason why people don't have what they want in life - but it's also not the number one reason.

The answer is – the biggest reason people don't have what they want in life yet is because THEY DON'T KNOW WHAT THEY WANT!

Roger had a former student of his as a client. The first session did not go well to say the least. This young man came "desperate for some direction" as he put it. He wanted advice on what steps he should next take, because he didn't have what he wanted in life.

OK. So he was asked directly "Just exactly what do you want in life?"

"Not sure really," was his answer.

That answer made it very hard – make that it made it impossible – for anybody to help him. The first step before asking anybody for directions when you are lost is to know where the hell it is that you want to go! Nobody can help you get what you want if you can't tell them what you want - because you don't know yourself.

He was told to do the following exercise before he came back for his follow-up. We'd like you to do it too.

Exercise No. 5: Create a story board for your life. Take time to clearly write your life's mission and goals out. Use photos if you like and state exactly what you want your ideal life to look like.

Jim, Chris and Roger have a ton of experience in business and in sports. They are all very fortunate to have followed their passions and created exciting and fruitful careers for themselves. And in their role now as TEAMMATES Personal Development Coaches, they are happy to help other people navigate the path to the kind of life and career they want to have for themselves.

But Roger cut his first session with his young student short and assigned Exercise No. 5 to his client; not because he was angry with him, but because he couldn't help him. Your GPS will not guide you properly if you don't put an address into it first.

This young man was trying to launch "a career in sports media in some way" for himself and wanted to tap into our expertise for that. That's why we're here we told him. Happy to help! But without a specific and clear vision for where he wanted to go in his career, we couldn't provide the proper direction.

If his vision was to be an on-air broadcaster, then his focus should be on getting the reps on camera. He would have to find ways to get in front of the camera, even as a volunteer, to hone his presentation skills.

If his vision was to be more behind the scenes, then he needed to focus on getting a job anywhere in the newsroom, doing any job to start out with, so he could work his way up in the organization. It wouldn't be necessary to get on-camera reps to do that.

If his vision was not media but working for a sports team, he needed to start with a local school team or small league's sports team, and learn the ropes that way while working his way up.

The problem was without a clear vision, there was no way for us to properly steer him in the right direction. Now many clients are just the opposite – they know exactly what they want. Great! For them, we help them formulate a plan to get it and encourage them to chase down their vision like they were running after the last bus of the night!

Those people with a specific vision are much easier to guide properly than someone who is just drifting. It's all right to spend time exploring different avenues until you develop your vision, but you aren't going to get what you want in life if you don't know what you want.

Many people spend more time planning their ideal vacations than they do planning what their ideal life is going to look like. Having a vision for your dream vacation is fun, but having a vision for the other 50 weeks of the year is far more important.

Take some time this week to really think about what EXACTLY you are looking for. What does your ideal life look like? Story boards are great, complete with pictures, but use the format that works best for you. Make it as specific as possible. Really attempt to see what your ideal life looks like and when you have that vision spelled out so that you can almost taste it and feel it - then you are ready to map your plan.

What are you doing for your career? Where are you living? How much money are you making? What specifically about your developing vision is making you excited and motivated enough to do whatever it takes to make it happen? Without that clear picture in mind, you may spend a lot of time heading down a road that's leading you further away from where you really want to go.

Develop a clear vision. You'll believe it when you see it!

WISDOM NUGGET #27: The biggest reason people don't have what they want in life is – they don't know what they want.

PRINCIPLE NO. 6: Be Flexible With Your Plans

Hopefully you are starting to notice that these Principles lead into each other. Principle No. 5 told you to develop a vision and that requires proper planning.

So Principle No. 6 is all about what to do with that plan. You developed a vision, you are working with your Personal Development Coach to make it happen and it's working! You are determined to follow that plan to the letter no matter what so success will be yours!

Wrong.

We have seen many clients in the past get off of the course they set for themselves. They worked hard at formulating a solid plan, started working it, and then veered off in a completely different direction. For some of them, this was a bad development as they just didn't follow through on what was a very good plan. For some others, however, the change in their plans was the best thing that could have happened to them.

Planning is important. The plan isn't.

Jim, Chris and Roger are big sports guys. All three of them have worked extensively in the sports world, and all three of them are massive sports fans to boot – which is why they all feel so satisfied with how their careers turned out.

One of the many great things about watching sports, or working in sports, or just observing sports, is what you can learn from them that you can use in every walk of life.

Several of our recommended reading books were penned by sports coaches. They are great books, because the lessons that terrific coaches like John Wooden and Phil Jackson can teach all of us are incredibly valuable. And one of the things all great sports coaches know is this – planning is crucial to success.

If you are going to win on the field, or on the court, or on the ice, you need to plan properly. The truly great coaches are great motivators but they are also excellent at "x's and o's" – drawing up complicated game plans to be able to stop their opponents from doing what they want to do.

Bill Belichick, the great head coach of the New England Patriots, is considered a master planner. His attention to detail is legendary and when he has extra time to prepare for an opponent, he's almost unbeatable. Nobody prepares like he does for next week's game.

But here's what he's also good at; making adjustments and being flexible with those plans. For example, let's say his game plan involved throwing the ball a lot. But during the first half, his (former) starting quarterback Tom Brady suffers a minor arm injury. Should he stubbornly continue with his original plan?

Hell no! He adjusts on the fly. Circumstances have changed. So even though he spent hundreds of hours on a plan that centers on Brady throwing the ball a great deal, he's going to abandon the plan because circumstances have changed.

This isn't just about having a Plan B ready, or a Plan C or D; it's acknowledging that any great plan requires some degree of flexibility. The goal of the Patriots is to win the game, not to run the original game plan no matter what happens.

Circumstances can change in a lot of different ways on a football field. Maybe the forecast changes dramatically, so that calls for more conservative play calling then planned. Somebody on the coach's team, or on the opposing team, gets hurt. That changes the landscape. Things can happen to alter the best approach a coach should take in order to win the game.

The point is, the Patriots stay committed to their goals of winning the game, but they stay flexible in their approach on how to win it.

Failing to plan in life is planning to fail. We know that. And the process of planning is crucial to success, and proper planning makes the chances of victory that much higher. We know that too.

But when Tom Brady steps back into the pocket and notices two receivers left wide open by the opposition, chances are the plan he had to run the ball down the middle changes. He calls an audible! The ultimate goal is not to follow the plan; the ultimate goal is to win the football game. Plans can't be so rigid that there is no room for a change in direction when necessary. That logic applies off the football field as well.

Try this exercise the next time you are in the midst of planning anything of importance in your life.

Exercise No. 6: Do proper planning for something in your life that you really want to go well. Be detailed. Then pretend something completely changed and think about how you would handle it.

We had a client once who was detailed obsessive about everything in her life. For the most part this was an admirable trait that served her well. Until her wedding day that is.

She had everything organized to a T. Every detail was meticulously crafted for the perfect outdoor wedding. Just one thing – the forecast was calling for a 100 percent chance of rain! But everything was planned; hundreds of hours were spent on the outdoor party. She became so fixated with nothing stopping her plan of the perfect outdoor wedding, she waited much too long to finally call "an audible" and take the party inside. Just ask the drenched guests that were there!

For good things of any kind in life to happen, proper planning is important. Things always go much better when proper plans are in place. But don't ever let your love of planning supersede your love of getting the results that you want. Plans sometimes change because they need to. Always keep the big picture in mind.

"Stay committed to your decisions, but stay flexible in your approach," says Tony Robbins. That's great advice.

Planning and preparation are very important. But the plan itself is not.

PRINCIPLE NO. 7: Embrace Failure

Put your hand up if you like to fail.

Don't see any hands. Well you are smart. Hey who likes to fail? It's never a fun experience when you fail at anything.

So you may have some problems with this next exercise in our seventh TEAMMATES Principle, which is going to ask you to embrace failure.

OK... most of us can understand that failure is just a part of the process of being in the game of life. We can learn to tolerate failure. We can learn to recover from failure. We can learn to persevere in spite of failure. But we are going one step beyond that because we think you should EMBRACE failure.

Whoa. That's another level entirely isn't it? But that is what Personal Development Coaching helps you do in a nutshell – take your life to the next level in every aspect. So let's see how we can do that with the concept of embracing failure when it comes. Try out this exercise this week.

Exercise No. 7: Take some time to study a situation where you failed. Break it all down. Accept it. Now be grateful for it and vow to use it to learn.

Those of our clients who are older generally find this exercise not as difficult as some of our younger clients do. There is a good reason for that – they have failed a lot more often and therefore really understand the value in failure! Young people sometimes struggle mightily with the first major failure that they experience, as it is new to them. But the longer you live and the more things you do, the more times you will fail…and in retrospect, you'll realize not only was the failure tolerable in the big picture of your life, it was often necessary.

Our blog on failure earlier in this book discusses this concept. We wrote about some major business failures and in particular United States President Abraham Lincoln, who encountered failure after failure before finally ascending to the highest office in the country. And we are all familiar with Thomas Edison's story of the 10,000 failures he had before he finally invented the light bulb. He never looked at any of the failed attempts as failures; he looked at them just as ways of him getting closer to accomplishing his goal.

But applying the lessons of these stories to our own lives is sometimes difficult. It is one thing to slap a friend on the back and tell them they can learn from this, it is another thing to do that for ourselves.

For Exercise No. 7, we really want you to break down a failure you had. To help you do that thoroughly, let's talk about the masters of analyzing failure – the airline industry.

In our recommended reading section there is a book by Matthew Syed called Black Box Thinking. It is brilliant. In it Syed talks about how when an airplane crashes, the search immediately begins for the black box, which contains all of the flight data.

Once that black box is found, it is analyzed in every possible way to determine the cause of the crash. The goal is to definitively find out what happened, and when that is determined, the work begins to correct the flaws that caused the crash in hope that it never happens again.

Syed suggests that this "Black Box Thinking" mentality should be applied to all walks of life, especially in the way it starts.

Once the black box is discovered, the analyzing starts in earnest. For a period of several weeks, everyone involved with the incident is encouraged to participate in finding out the causes of the crash with complete immunity. In other words – they do not have to fear being blamed for the crash, as the goal is not to find fault but to find solutions to make sure it never happens again.

As a result of that mentality, many terrible crashes have led to new rules, new formats, and new equipment – whatever is needed – to make air travel safer. The failure is not shunned, it is not tolerated, it is not condemned… it is embraced, because of what can be learned from it.

Syed compares that to the medical profession. When a patient dies, what generally happens sadly is that tracks are covered up. Nobody wants to be held responsible for a death. There are fears of lawsuits all around. The end result – there is no black box thinking with full immunity applied. The fear of blame (which might lead to those potential lawsuits), is greater than the desire to discover what lead to the death, in order that something can be learned by it.

The medical profession needs to instill the same black box mentality when it comes to tragic events as the airline profession has. As an example, a nurse should have no fear of saying he or she made a mistake, or calling out a doctor error, or "throwing somebody under the bus" for procedural mistakes. The point of black box thinking is not to find blame; it is to find causes so that steps can be taken to make sure similar situations do not occur again. Honest assessments done immediately after a tragedy can lead to the saving of lives in the future. However that doesn't happen when people are focused on just trying to avoid being blamed.

This is what we want you to do with a failure you have experienced in your life; recover the black box so to speak. Really dig into the causes of what led to the failure. Analyze it fully – not to find blame with yourself or someone else, but to discover what exactly happened so you can take steps to ensure similar failures in your own life never happen again.

As you get older you realize that you do indeed learn more from defeat than from victory. Your failures are better teachers than your successes. Your bad times give you more knowledge than your good times do.

One of our young clients really struggled with this concept.

"I cannot love the fact that I failed, that's impossible!" he told us.

He missed the point. We are not asking you to love the failure, we are asking you to embrace it and use black box thinking to find the reasons for it. When your "investigation" is complete, you will be able to use the data to make sure you don't fail in the same way ever again.

When you learn to embrace failure, you may indeed find out that in retrospect, it turned out to be the best thing that could have happened to you. That thought is very difficult to fathom when the failure first occurs, but it is easier to understand after some inspection into why you failed.

Apply black box thinking to your failures. Win or learn!

PRINCIPLE NO. 8: Stay Focused

Multitasking is passé.

Sorry to break that piece of news to you, especially those of you that like to juggle three things at once, but it has been proven many times that dividing our attention to detail makes our work sloppier, and multitasking does not make us more efficient.

The entire mindfulness movement was what really changed the perception of multitasking. Working on answering emails, taking a call, eating a sandwich and painting your house at the same time was once considered a badge of honor. It is now considered pretty foolish, which is a good thing.

Focus. On. One. Thing. At. A. Time.

Give it a try this week by working through the following exercise.

Exercise No. 8: Take an hour to zero in on one task. Doesn't matter what it is, but totally dedicate your attention to it 100% - like Tiger Woods does in the following story. Set a timer. See if you feel more productive.

One our favorite stories about the power of focus involves one of the greatest athletes of all time, the legendary golfer Tiger Woods.

Our No. 8 Principle is to stay focused, and there was never anybody in his prime who could stay as focused as Tiger could, as the following story illustrates.

Legendary hockey coach Scotty Bowman is a big golf fan. He even worked as an official at some PGA tournaments in Florida, wearing a uniform on the course. Scotty is also a friend of Tiger Woods.

Bowman found out he would be working at a tournament Tiger was playing in, but didn't have a chance to let him know prior. As he arrived at the course and was changing, Bowman told the other scorekeepers and minor officials that Tiger would be shocked when he saw him. He told them he was a great friend of Tiger's and he couldn't wait to see how Tiger reacted to seeing him – a hockey coach - in such an unfamiliar role. Tiger had no idea that Bowman was working this particular tournament.

As the round was about to start, Bowman stood in his designated position at the first tee. Woods walked past him, nodded and went about his business. The other officials chuckled at Scotty.

"He barely acknowledged you," one said. "You sure you guys are friends?!"

Bowman assured him that they were, but through the 18 holes Tiger never said a word to him or even cracked a smile. Bowman had a job to do, and Tiger was playing an important round of golf, but Scotty was still a little disappointed that his friend didn't even say hello once. The other officials teased him, wondering out loud if Tiger Woods even knew who Scotty Bowman was, never mind being his pal!

The round ends. Everyone heads to the official scorer's tent, including Tiger to sign his scorecard. Once he signs his card the round is officially over. Players and officials can then finally relax.

Tiger signs his scorecard and then looks up and sees Scotty standing with a few other officials.

"Scotty Bowman!" Tiger yelled with a laugh. "What the hell are you doing here?! When did you come in?"

Tiger greeted Scotty warmly, talked with the other officials, and chatted like they were best of friends. Tiger never noticed Scotty before that moment, even though Scotty says he directly looked at Tiger numerous times during the round.

"He never saw me, he was that focused on his round," Bowman remembers. "He only saw me for the first time when the round was over and his focus was turned off."

Focus. Tiger Woods is famous for it. He's not out on the course to see friends, or swat at a fly, or to admire the scenery. He is out there to win a golf tournament. He is zeroed in on one task only.

A great book on this topic is Flow by Mihaly Csikszentmihalyi. In it he outlines how athletes, entertainers, and other people from every walk of life reach the optimal state of Flow when they are fully engaged in the task they are working on.

Time stops for them. They become completely immersed in their task. They are in a state of Flow.

Reaching that stage allows them to hit optimal performance. Everything else drifts away, and all of their energies are engaged in what they are doing. It is a beautiful thing to watch when you see someone in the zone like that.

Flow is really just heightened focus and it is something we can all achieve with practice. You might have already experienced it; have you ever worked on something and looked up at a clock and realized two hours went by? How sometimes time seems to fly by instead of drag? You are in Flow when that happens. It's when many of us produce our best work.

It is not easy in this day and age to stay focused. Modern life has so many distractions it throws at us on an hourly basis. That's why we recommend this exercise to help you work on developing your ability to really focus when you need to.

Turn off your phone. Put your device on airplane mode. Put all of your energies into the task you are doing and if you find yourself drifting, get right back to it.

Sounds a little like meditating doesn't it? It's really mindfulness and living in the moment practiced fully. Do one thing at a time and see how much better you do that thing.

Stay focused now. Just two more Principles for us to cover!

> WISDOM NUGGET #28: Stay totally focused on your goals. Think of the power of a magnifying glass in the sun burning a piece of paper!

PRINCIPLE NO. 9: Define YOUR Success

What is success?

Of all the questions you will ask during your life's journey, this is the one that is the most important for you to answer.

An earlier TEAMMATES Principle was about having a vision, and this one is similar. Remember what we said was the biggest reason people didn't have what they want? It's because they don't know what they want. And in the same vein, the biggest reason people don't achieve the success they want is that they haven't properly defined what success is for them.

What is success? We cannot answer that question for you, because the definition of success is different for everyone. Only you have the answer to what success means for you.

> **Exercise No. 9: Write your Life Mission Statement. Take some time with this. In ONE sentence, what do you stand for and what do you want? How do you define success?**

One of Roger's first clients was a lawyer who was a friend of his. This man was so unhappy that eventually he went into therapy for his issues, which he fortunately later came to terms with.

The Personal Development Coaching sessions were difficult for this client. On the surface, this man had a lot going for him and was very successful. He was a partner in his law firm, he was very wealthy, and he was married with two children living in a beautiful home. He appeared to be the definition of success.

Ah but here's the point – by whose definition?

He was a great lawyer by all accounts. There was just one thing – he hated being a lawyer. And I mean he HATED being a lawyer, as he confided to Roger.

From the time he started law school, he determined that law was not something he was passionate about. Nonetheless, he shined in the classroom, got his accreditation, and became "wildly successful" in the law field.

During his time working with Roger he split up with his wife and he left their family home. It was then that he decided he needed therapy, not just some coaching.

His story has a happy ending though. He resolved his issues and is in a much better place today. But his situation was a great learning experience for Roger to us with future clients – it demonstrated how important knowing what your 'Why' was.

Why are YOU living the way you are living now? What is your motivation? Why do you get out of bed in the morning?

Many of us think we know our "Why" but we really don't. We haven't dug deep enough yet to really understand why we are doing the things we are doing. For instance – are you presently working as an actor because you really love acting, or are you doing it because you like the fame it brings you? If it's the latter you may feel yourself getting more and more disinterested in your profession as the years go by.

Our client became a lawyer in the first place not because he loved law, but because he felt the need to make a lot of money for his family and becoming a lawyer was a way he could do that. The more successful he became, the more money he made. However the time he spent in the building of his practice resulted in him never being home, so he drifted apart from his family as a result.

How sad. The very reason he wanted to be a lawyer in the first place – to provide for his family – wound up costing him his family. His priorities were amiss.

All major businesses have a mission statement. Some are as short as one sentence, others a few paragraphs, but the good ones are as succinct as possible. We want you to write your own Life Statement Mission.

This is not at all easy for some people, but it is a tremendous exercise in determining what success you should go after. What does success look like for you? You need to define that before you begin trying to get that success.

You should always be honest with people, but the most important person to be honest with is yourself. Don't hedge your bets with this exercise – if you want something say it clearly. What exactly does success look like to you?

The story of the young man on the fishing boat in Blog No. 6 is a favorite of ours. Go back and read it again. What is the point of "having it all" if you can't enjoy it all? What is the point of having the biggest home on the block if you never have the time to be in it? We spend far too much time trying to impress people we don't like instead of just doing the things we want to do.

It comes down to this. Live your values. What is most important to you? And WHY is it most important to you? A man is truly a success if he has lived the kind of life he wants to live, and not the kind of life that someone else wants him to live.

Write your mission statement. Live your values. Much success to you!

PRINCIPLE NO. 10: Passion. Preparation. PERSISTENCE!

Let's call these the Three P's To Success.

Jim, Chris and Roger have had different careers, but there are some similarities. All three of them have been heavily involved in the sports world, and all three of them have done some teaching.

Teachers like to leave students with something that's makes it easy to remember a lesson by. So for our final TEAMMATES Principle, let us discuss the Three Ps to successful personal development – Passion. Preparation. PERSISTENCE.

Persistence is in all caps for a good reason. It is the most important aspect of long-term success.

It takes a lot of different attributes to succeed. Hard work, talent and a bit of luck are certainly three of them. However our experience has shown that the hard working, talented people seem to get all the luck. Funny how that works out, hey friends?!

We've all heard the adage of how hard work beats talent when talent doesn't work hard. That is also true, as is especially demonstrated in the sports world. So work hard, develop your talent, you'll get some luck and off you go then? It's really that simple?

We think there's a little more to it than that, and that's where the Three P's come in.

Passion.

You don't have to be passionate about something to succeed in it. But it sure helps.

We are told to follow our passion from the time we are children. It is great advice. Do what you love we are told. Of course you should.

Yet as we get older and "reality" sets in, our passions get harder to follow, don't they? We are told "there's no money in that line of work" or "that field is too crowded" or "you have to go to school forever to do that, is it worth it?" And so, quite often, our passion gets buried.

Follow your passion by all means. And if you don't have something you are passionate about yet, that's OK. But keep searching for that thing you most love to do, and then go out and start doing it.

Is passion NECESSARY for great success? Sometimes it is not. There are some people that can have pretty decent careers without being passionate about what they do.

Notice we say "pretty decent" however, and not "great."

Do you want to be mediocre, or do you want to be great? You can have some degree of success doing something without passion, but the truly great at anything are absolutely passionate about what they do.

A good example is seen when you watch an athlete train. Their passion really comes out then. They are so passionate about their careers that they work harder and work longer than those that don't have a similar passion. The same is true in the business world. The passionate people are the ones who become the superstars in all fields.

When you have a passion for what you are doing, the work you do is made easier. It's more fun. You want to get at it in the morning; it is what drives you. So the first 'P' is definitely passion. Find what you love to do and go out there and do it with passion.

Preparation.

A lot of people like the idea of being an actor. Not very many people like the idea of going to acting school to become one however.

Abraham Lincoln, who you read about in one of our blogs, said "Give me six hours to chop down a tree and I will spend the first four sharpening the axe." Honest Abe sure knew the value of preparation.

One of our clients is a golf instructor. He has a huge pet peeve about many of the people he coaches. They head out to the course and can't wait to get on the first tee. Some of them get right out there and start their round, after maybe only taking a few stretches before they hit their first shot.

It drives him crazy to see that! He equates it to hockey, football and baseball; what do the players do in those sports just prior to playing a game? They warm up properly. They prepare. Yet some amateur golfers expect to have great success in their rounds with almost no warm-up or preparation for it. Our client insists that they hit some balls on the practice tee before they tee off for their rounds.

The will to win is quite common. The will to prepare to win is not so common.

Malcolm Gladwell's book Outliers advocated the theory that to become an expert at anything requires 10,000 hours of practice and preparation. While that exact number has been the subject of much conjecture, the principle behind it isn't. Overnight success does not happen overnight. It never has and it never will.

You either prepare to win or you prepare to fail. So the second 'P' to success is without question Preparation.

PERSISTENCE!

This is the most important attribute to success, so much so it deserves to be put in all caps. PERSISTENCE!

It is also the one that cannot be taught. This TEAMMATES Personal Development Coaching program cannot teach this to you and neither can anybody else. It is the one thing you have to bring to the table on your own.

The good news is PERSISTENCE is not a talent; it is an attitude. Anybody can decide they are going to be persistent. Of the Three P's to success it is the most vital one to acquire. And only you can give it to yourself.

You've taken this course. You've read the blogs and listened to the tape. You know what you need to do to have a great life. Now – are you going to do our last exercise?

"Nothing in this world can take the place of persistence. Talent will not; nothing is more common than unsuccessful men with talent. Genius will not; unrewarded genius is almost a proverb. Education will not; the world is full of educated derelicts. Persistence and determination alone are omnipotent. The slogan 'Press On!' has solved and always will solve the problems of the human race."
— ***Calvin Coolidge***

Exercise No. 10: CAUTION: This exercise takes time. We want you to work on achieving your life goals and be happy while you do it. Please do this exercise for the rest of your life.

WISDOM NUGGET #29: Nothing life changing happens overnight; patience is waiting for the seeds you planted to bloom.

CONCLUSION (or is it?)

When you come to the end, it will be the beginning.

Our course is ending now, but here is where you begin to apply the principles we have discussed in our blogs, in our podcasts and in this book. So it isn't the end, it is just the beginning.

One thing that separates TEAMMATES from other self-help programs is the large amount of personal coaching that comes along with our book and audio product. Many of you who have taken the course have already been working with our Personal Development Coaches; they will continue to work with you moving forward as you apply the principles we have discussed throughout this program. We are now true TEAMMATES and we are delighted to be on your team moving forward. If you have used this book on your own, thank you for reading and feel free to reach out anytime to explore our Personal Development Coaching program. If you are working with another mentor, we wish you much success as well.

It would be nice and neat right now for all of us if we could just have a tidy summary for everything - wouldn't it? If we could boil everything we've discussed here down to a paragraph, or even a page, so it would be compact and simple to remember. Especially in this day and age - who has the time to sit down and read 2,000 books, or study for 10,000 hours, or listen to hundreds of hours of self-improvement tapes?

One of our favorite clients once told us in a frustrated tone: "I don't have time for any self-improvement exercises. I am just trying to get through the day!"

Aren't we all?

So this "Conclusion" will not even attempt to give you all your answers in one spot. If we could do that we wouldn't have taken the hundreds of hours we did to put this course together for you in the first place. But any work of this length deserves to have a bow put on it so to speak, so let's do that for you.

Jim, Chris and Roger all have signature taglines, as those of you who have followed TEAMMATES from the start are well aware of.

"Best always" says Jim.

"BE OUTSTANDING!" says Chris.

"Look for Good!" says Roger.

I guess we could leave it at that. You should always give it your best. You should always strive to be outstanding. You should look for the good in every situation. We are certainly willing to hang our hats on our taglines… we use them all the time after all!

But what you really took this course for is – you want to know HOW to do those things.

How do you give your best always? How do you be outstanding? How do you learn to always look for good?

We are confident in saying that taking this course was a very positive first step for you in being able to do those things. If you embraced the program fully, answered all the questions, read the blogs, listened to the audio program, read this book to the end – congratulations. You are on the way to making your life much better by investing time in personal development and growth.

You have shown a commitment to be better – and that commitment will pay dividends for you moving forward.

But we promised you a quick summary. So here it is:

Remember the Top 10 TEAMMATES Principles:

1. Be grateful. Have an attitude of gratitude.
2. Live in the moment. We only have moments to live after all.
3. Choose optimism. You can control how you look at things.

4. **Have a growth mindset. Train your brain for success-ful thinking.**
5. **Have a vision. Picture exactly what it is you want.**
6. **Be flexible. Planning is important the plan itself isn't.**
7. **Embrace failure. Practice black box thinking.**
8. **Stay focused. One day at a time, one thing at a time.**
9. **Define your success. Live your values.**
10. **Passion, Preparation, PERSISTENCE! Press On!**

One final story if we may before you press on with your life...

There was a village that was ruled by elders. They had all the wisdom the village members needed to survive and they guarded that wisdom very carefully. But they didn't trust the younger members of the village with having access to this wisdom, for fear of what they would do with it.

They were convinced that the youngsters would misuse it or worse still, destroy it.

They gathered as a group to decide what they would do.

"We must hide the wisdom from the young," one of the elders told the meeting. "It must be protected at all costs."

There was agreement all around. But the question remained, where do they hide it?

"Bury it by the river; it is a sacred spot for our village. The young never go there anymore," one said.

"They are too smart. They will think of that and discover it," said another.

"Then hide it in the forest," said another. "It is so large it will be impossible to find in there."

"They have modern tools that can help them search far and wide," answered an elder in the back. "They will surely hunt it down and find it there."

There was much consternation among the elders. They did not think the young should be given the wisdom as they would abuse it – but they had no idea where a safe place might be to hide it from them.

Finally the oldest elder of them all, a tiny frail ancient woman, slowly came to the front of the room and wished to be heard. Everyone listened.

"There is only one safe place to hide the wisdom from the young," the woman slowly said.

With baited breath everyone waited for her solution.

"Just hide the wisdom inside of them," she said. "That is the one place they will never look for it."

You may not have everything you want in life yet but you have everything you need. The answers to the questions you have on how to live a great life are all sitting inside of you. There are many general principles that can help you, but instead of looking outside of yourself for wisdom, we suggest that you look inside.

We are all searching for answers on how to have a better life. We look long and far; we read many books, we listen to many tapes, and we study from reliable personal development coaches to gain the tools and skills we need to acquire knowledge to be better.

That is a good thing to do. This course will help you to gain some very valuable knowledge that will help in your journey, as will many other courses and books.

But nobody can teach you wisdom. That will come from inside of you after you have made the efforts to really ask yourself what you want, and how you want to get it. The greatest source of wisdom on how you should live your life does not come from the outside, it comes from within.

Live your values friends. Define your own success. Live how you want to live.

The course is now over…but it's really just the beginning. It is time for you to go out there and live it. Thank you for trusting us to help you discover the greatest self-development principle of all:

The only thing that is stopping you from being everything you want to be in life…is you.

Blessings,
Jim, Chris and Roger

WISDOM NUGGET #30: You don't have to change
your whole life; you just have to change
how you look at it.

RECOMMENDED READING

The best way to learn is to read. There are many excellent books out there that can be useful in your personal development.

In addition to the self-help book industry, there are many business books, biographies and other books that can enrich your mind and help make you a better person. We believe the ones that are the most useful are those based more on scientific principles than on "pop psychology" but as you will see from this list, there is a wide variety of material we would like to recommend. A great deal of the information we use in our TEAMMATES course comes from these and other books that span more than a century between publication.

Jim, Chris and Roger have read an awful lot of books over the years. They learned a lot from them. But reading 2,000 books takes a lot of time, so they have listed just some of the best ones here that are definitely worth a read to assist you on your own journey.

As is the case with almost anything, personal preference comes into play in what anyone finds valuable to read. But as is discussed in our audio program, we cannot emphasize enough the importance of giving your mind a workout in the same way you give one to your body. Most books offer some degree of value and it is better to read a book you enjoy (either because of the writer or the style of writing), rather than to read a book just because you think you should.

Good books are to your mind what good food is to your body; the proper nutrients in both cases will improve your mental and physical health. So be as careful with what you put into your mind as you are with what you would put into your body.

Our recommended books are listed alphabetically by author's last name:

- **James Allen**: Mind is the Master, Complete works
- **Maya Angelou**: Rainbow in the Cloud
- **Kenneth Blanchard & Spencer Johnson**: The One Minute Manager
- **Claude M. Bristol**: The Magic of Believing
- **David Burns**: Feeling Good: The New Mood Therapy
- **Rhonda Byrne**: The Secret
- **Jack Canfield**: The Success Principles
- **Richard Carlson**: Don't Sweat The Small Stuff
- **Dale Carnegie**: How to Stop Worrying and Start Living
- **Deepak Chopra**: Creating Affluence
- **Paulo Coelho**: The Alchemist
- **Geoff Colvin**: Talent is Overrated
- **Norman Cousins**: The Anatomy of an Illness
- **Stephen Covey**: Everyday Greatness
- **Pat Croce**: 110%
- **Mihaly Csikszentmihalyi**: Flow
- **Dr. Joe Dispenza**: You Are The Placebo
- **Dr. Joe Dispenza**: Evolve Your Brain
- **Dr. Joe Dispenza**: Becoming Supernatural
- **Dr. Joe Dispenza**: Breaking The Habit of Being Yourself
- **Mark Divine**: The Way of the Seal
- **Angela Duckworth**: GRIT
- **Wayne Dyer**: Change Your Thoughts Change Your Life
- **Wayne Dyer**: A New Way of Thinking, A New Way of Being
- **David Epstein**: The Sports Gene
- **Tim Ferriss**: Tools of Titans
- **Debbie Ford**: The Best Year of Your Life
- **Viktor Frankl**: Man's Search for Meaning
- **Shakti Gawain**: Creative Visualization
- **Malcolm Gladwell**: Outliers
- **Seth Godin**: Purple Cow
- **Thomas Harris**: I'm OK You're OK
- **Jerry & Esther Hicks**: The Essential Law of Attraction Collection

- **Napoleon Hill**: Think and Grow Rich
- **Lou Holtz**: Winning Every Day
- **Phil Jackson**: Eleven Rings
- **Susan Jeffers**: Feel the Fear and Do It Anyway
- **Spencer Johnson**: Who Moved My Cheese?
- **Jon Kabat-Zinn**: Full Catastrophe Living
- **Jon Kabat-Zinn**: Wherever You Go There You Are
- **Ellen J. Langer**: Mindfulness
- **Og Mandino**: The Greatest Success in the World
- **John C. Maxwell**: How Successful People Think
- **Thich Nhat Hanh**: Happiness
- **Judith Orloff**: Emotional Freedom
- **Judith Orloff**: Positive Energy
- **Norman Vincent Peale**: The Power of Positive Thinking
- **Scott Peck**: The Road Less Traveled
- **Thomas L. Peters & Robert H. Waterman Jr.**: In Search of Excellence
- **Jordan B. Peterson**: 12 Rules for Life
- **Yongey Mingyur Rinpoche**: The Joy of Living
- **Anthony Robbins**: Unlimited Power
- **Jim Rohn**: 7 Strategies for Wealth and Happiness
- **Robert H. Schuller**: Tough Times Never Last, But Tough People Do
- **Martin E.P. Seligman**: Learned Optimism
- **Martin E.P. Seligman**: Flourish
- **Martin E.P. Seligman**: Authentic Happiness
- **Michael A. Singer**: The Untethered Soul
- **Matthew Syed**: Bounce
- **Matthew Syed**: Black Box Thinking
- **Richard H. Thaler & Cass R. Sunstein**: Nudge
- **Eckhart Tolle**: The Power of Now
- **Eckhart Tolle**: A New Earth
- **Brian Tracy**: Eat That Frog!
- **Denis Waitley**: The New Dynamics of Goal Setting
- **Bronnie Ware**: The Top Five Regrets of the Dying
- **Jack Welch**: Winning

- **Williams, Teasdale, Segal & Kabat-Zinn**: The Mindful Way Through Depression
- **Pat Williams**: Who Wants to be a Champion?
- **Pat Williams**: How to Be Like Coach Wooden
- **Oprah Winfrey**: What I Know For Sure
- **John Wooden**: A Game Plan For Life
- **Robert Wright**: Why Buddhism is True
- **Zig Ziglar**: Born to Win

ABOUT THE AUTHORS

CHRIS DE PIERO has been an educator in various forms for the past 26 years, as a teacher and coach. He has been the Director of Athletics at St. Michael's College School as well as a classroom teacher. He played professional hockey in Italy before becoming an accomplished hockey coach, leading the St. Michael's Buzzers to back-to-back Ontario titles before moving on to the Ontario Hockey League. Chris was Assistant Coach, Assistant General Manager, Head Coach and General Manager with the Oshawa Generals from 2006-12, and worked as an Amateur Scout for the Pittsburgh Penguins from 2012-16. He recently returned to North America after serving as Assistant Coach with Hockey Club Lugano in Switzerland, and is once again working for St. Michael's College School in an administrative role. BE OUTSTANDING!

JIM ROONEY has been a fixture in Guelph sports for decades. He was co-owner, president and governor of the Ontario Hockey League's Guelph Storm from 1991-2006, and Chairman of the Board of Governors of the OHL from 1995-2001. His Guelph teams won two OHL titles (1998, 2004) and participated in four Memorial Cups, including one as a host city. He later became owner of the Guelph Royals of the Intercounty Baseball League after serving as the league's Commissioner from 2001-2009. He was principal at Bishop Macdonell and Our Lady of Lourdes high schools, where many of his Guelph players attended. Jim was also co-chair of the Ontario Winter Games (2002-03), and was Educational Consultant for Team Canada's first U-18 gold medal winning team in Russia in 2003. He was elected to the Guelph Sports Hall of Fame in 2017 to recognize his outstanding contributions as a builder in Guelph sports over many decades. BEST ALWAYS!

ROGER LAJOIE has been working in the sports media field for more than four decades. He has been a reporter, editor, broadcaster, announcer, author, teacher and hockey executive at various times in his career. He taught at Ryerson University in the Sports Media program for four years and was a teacher at the College of Sports Media from 2008-18. He wrote the biography of Canadian hockey legend Paul Henderson among his three published books, and has done close to 4,000 shows as a radio talk show host on Sportsnet 590 The Fan. He has covered more than 250 major sporting events, including 17 World Series, 14 Stanley Cup Finals, 13 Super Bowls and 11 NBA Finals. He has worked as an executive for the Canadian Hockey League, and was Vice President of both the Mississauga St. Michael's Majors of the OHL and the Belleville Senators of the AHL. For 10 seasons he has been one of the Official Scorers of the Toronto Blue Jays and has operated Triumph Sports Communications for more than 30 years. He has been personal coaching/mentoring clients since 2013. LOOK FOR GOOD!

Printed in Canada